FIGHTING SHAME
WITH THE WORD OF GOD

ASHAMED

SCARLET HILTIBIDAL

Lifeway Press®
Brentwood, Tennessee

ISBN: 978-1-0877-8299-7
Item: 005841742
Dewey decimal classification: 248.843
Subject heading: WOMEN \ CHRISTIAN LIFE \ BIBLE--STUDY AND TEACHING

To order additional copies of this resource, write Lifeway Resources Customer Service; 200 Powell Place, Suite 100; Brentwood, TN 37027-7707; FAX order to 615.251.5933; call toll-free 800.458.2772; email orderentry@lifeway.com; or order online at *lifeway.com*.

Printed in the United States of America

Lifeway Resources
200 Powell Place, Suite 100
Brentwood, TN 37027-7707

TABLE OF CONTENTS

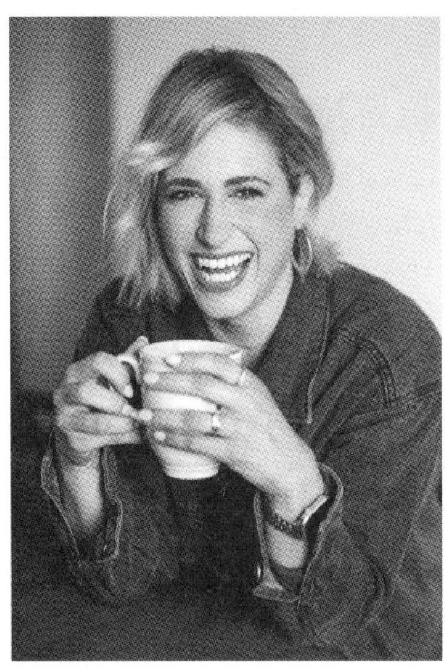

Photo: Courtney George with Fox Creative

ABOUT THE AUTHOR

Scarlet Hiltibidal is the author of *Afraid of All the Things, You're the Worst Person in the World, He Numbered the Pores on My Face*, and the Bible study *Anxious*. She writes regular columns for *ParentLife* and *HomeLife Magazines* and devotionals for *She Reads Truth* and enjoys speaking to women around the country about the freedom and rest available in Jesus. Scarlet has a degree in biblical counseling and taught elementary school before she started writing. She and her husband live in Tennessee where she loves communicating in sign language with her three daughters, eating nachos by herself, writing for her friends, and studying stand-up comedy with a passion that should be reserved for more important pursuits.

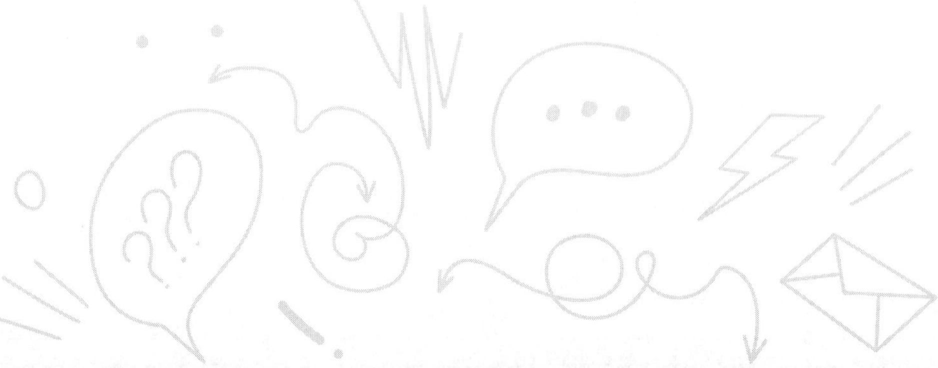

HOW TO USE THIS STUDY

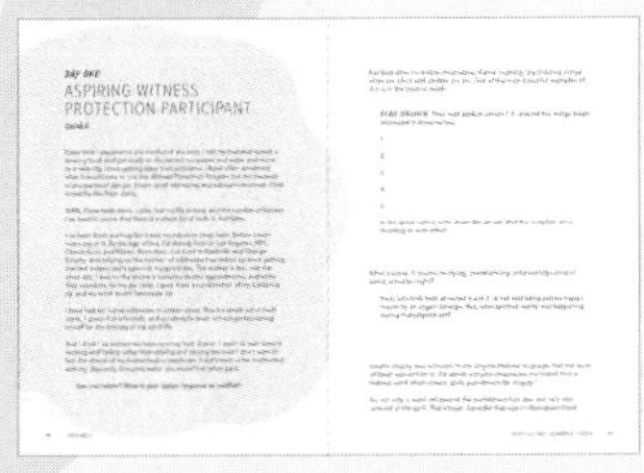
ASPIRING WITNESS PROTECTION PARTICIPANT

PERSONAL STUDY

Each week you'll have five days of personal study. You'll watch the video teaching after completing the five days of personal study. The first session is an introduction followed by the video teaching. If you're studying with a group, you can read the introduction together or on your own before you meet to watch the video and discuss.

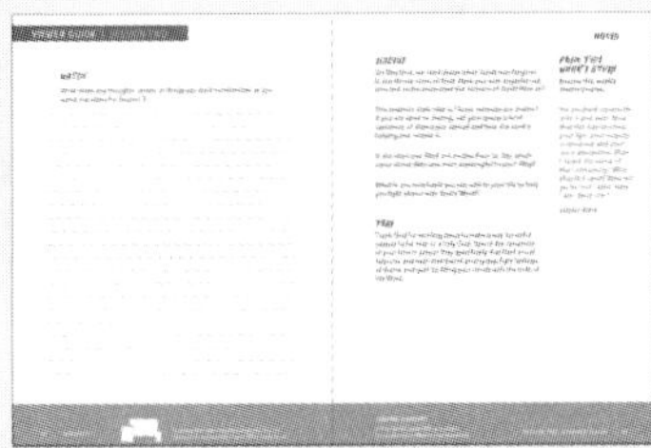

VIDEO VIEWER GUIDE

Each session of *Ashamed* ends with a teaching video from Scarlet. The Viewer Guide page provides you with a place to take notes from the video teachings and from your small group discussion time. You'll want to begin your study by reading the Introduction and then watching the Session One video and taking notes on page 12.

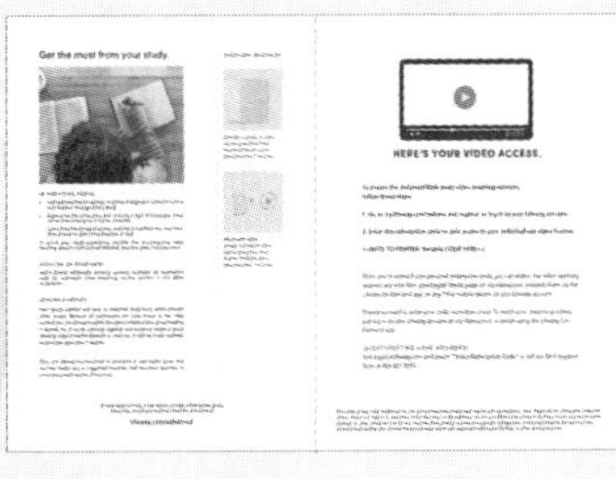
Get the most from your study

HERE'S YOUR VIDEO ACCESS.

VIDEO ACCESS

With the purchase of this book, you have access to videos from Scarlet that provide insight to help you better understand and apply what you study. You'll find detailed information on how to access the teaching videos on the card in the back of your Bible study book.

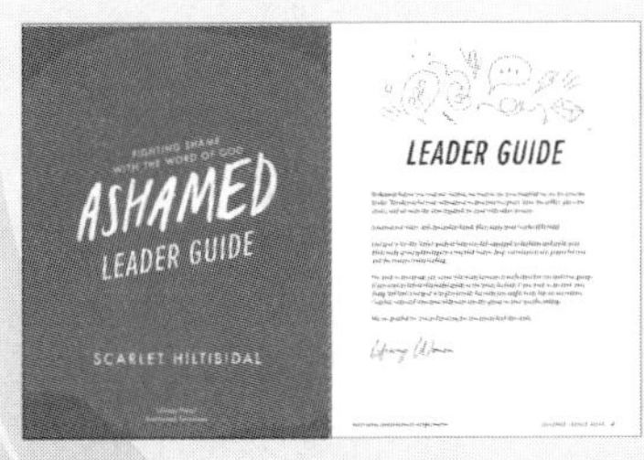

LEADING A GROUP?

A free leader guide PDF is available for download at **lifeway.com/ashamed**. The leader guide offers general tips and helps along with discussion guides for each week.

SESSION ONE

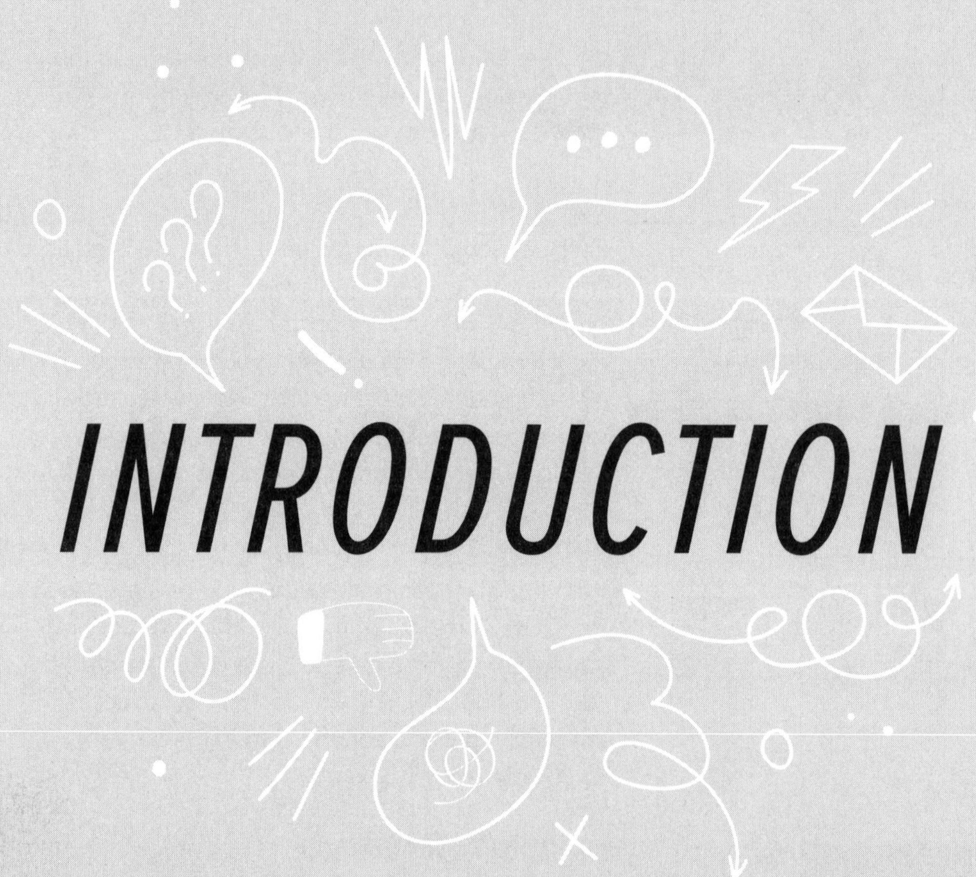

INTRODUCTION

MEMORY VERSE

THEN SAID I, WOE IS ME!
FOR I AM UNDONE;
BECAUSE I AM A MAN
OF UNCLEAN LIPS, AND
I DWELL IN THE MIDST OF
A PEOPLE OF UNCLEAN
LIPS: **FOR MINE EYES
HAVE SEEN THE KING,
THE LORD OF HOSTS.**

ISAIAH 6:5, KJV

(EMPHASIS ADDED)

INTRODUCTION

We often hear or see affirmations from well-meaning people telling us we are worthy. "You are amazing! You are beautiful! You are worthy!" You can see the Instagram® post now, can't you? And I so want it to be true. I want to be worthy. I want to be worthy of love, of comfort, of success, of a day at the spa, of all the good stuff and none of the bad stuff, please. Don't you want that, too?

My first several years walking with Jesus were marked by a panicked desperation to obtain that worthiness. I thought being worthy would lead to comfort. It sounds so nice to be worthy. I still sometimes think that way.

Like, I may not be worthy in this moment, but I *could* be worthy if I tried hard enough, right?

At the moment I'm writing this, I'm on a plane, headed across the country to speak to a group of women about Jesus. Surely someone who writes for and speaks to women about Jesus and the Bible needs to be worthy, right? Especially by the time I stand on a platform and talk about the most important and definitely worthy Person who has ever lived.

Don't worry, guys. I'll get worthy by then. The conference isn't until tomorrow afternoon anyway. So, maybe not the end of this day, but surely worthiness will happen to me before tomorrow afternoon.

Here's the thing. It won't. We know that. Worthiness won't arrive just by me thinking about worthiness.

To think of myself as "worthy" is to forget the cross. It doesn't work. And every time I get caught up in a cycle of striving and failing, of focusing on what I do more than what Jesus does, I end up feeling short-lived self-righteousness or feeling devastated by shame. I so want to be worthy, but I so often feel shame.

WHAT IS SHAME?

I think of shame as that horrible sinking feeling you get when you say the wrong thing, when you hurt someone you love, when you realize you've done wrong and there's nothing you can do to fix it. That *if I could just turn back the clock ten minutes* feeling. That feeling of, *Oh no, I've blown it all. The thing or the people or the life I love is irreparably broken.*

Oftentimes, we feel shame because of things we've done, but there are other reasons we can find ourselves feeling ashamed.

What about the woman who struggles to find a job or who just lost a job (a job that consumed her thoughts and her minutes and her ambitions)? What about the women who battle infertility or wrestle with body image? I think of Elizabeth's story, which you can read in Luke 1. Elizabeth, who couldn't control her inability to conceive and yet it was a source of shame for her. Shame in these situations may be cultural; it may not be the result of anything we've done but of circumstances beyond our control.

Or what about the shame you carry, not because of what you've done or not done, but because of what was done to you? Not the shame of your own sin, but the shame you carry because of how others have sinned against you.

You don't necessarily have to be the villain to feel like you are, right?

Additionally and heartbreakingly, there is a deep and difficult kind of shame resulting from physical and emotional abuse. We see a biblical example of this kind of shame in the life of Tamar (2 Sam. 13), who was raped. If you've walked through this sort of trauma, we encourage you to get support.*

Life is so hard. From the most extreme to the most "minor," we have all felt humiliated, embarrassed, and ashamed.

Shame is a sad reality in our broken world, especially when it plagues those of us who are in Christ. We weren't meant to live in hopelessness, crushed under the weight of shame.

* To find a professional counselor in your area, you might want to check out websites like aacc.net, focusonthefamily.com/counseling, and biblicalcounseling.com, or ask your pastor or church leader for their recommendations. If you are currently in an abusive situation, please reach out to your local authorities or call the National Domestic Violence Hotline at 800.799.7233. There are people who can help you get into a place of safety.

HOPE FOR THE SHAMED

A long time ago, the prophet Isaiah stepped into the throne room of God, and he was "undone" by his brokenness in view of God's holiness. His response was a cry of despair and a recognition that he shouldn't have even been alive in the presence of such perfection. But then, a weird and beautiful thing happened—a terror-inducing angel, through the smoke and the shaking and the grandeur, touched Isaiah's mouth with a coal and told him his sin was forgiven. Isaiah's response? HERE I AM. SEND ME. I DON'T CARE. I'M YOURS! I'LL DO WHATEVER! That is the explosive beauty at the core of the Christian experience. Isaiah moved from death to life. He moved from being undone by shame to having a hopeful humility and an urgency to serve the Lord.

You guys, this is what Jesus does.

We were as good as dead, but the forgiveness of God gives us new life, new purpose, new confidence, new hope.

Unfortunately, many people never experience undoneness. Countless women and men move through life convincing themselves they are the source of grandeur and hope. That doesn't work either. God's design for the human heart is to encounter its own unworthiness, see God as glorious and gracious, and leave all self-sufficiency and shame behind as we trust in Him. Anything else leaves us hopelessly fighting to prove to ourselves and the world that we are worthy, when deep down we know we still won't be when the plane lands.

So, what are we doing here? Why are you doing this Bible study? Circle which of the two categories below you think you fall into.

IF YOU'RE UNDONE (OR NEED TO BE)

If you fear that you need to have your life together to participate in a Bible study, don't worry. It's actually the opposite. This is for undone people (and people who need to be undone). To be undone, in the case of Isaiah, is to realize your own unworthiness in the presence of the One who is worthy. The right amount of undoneness is good for us; it leads to humility and trust in God. I pray that this Bible study helps you see and remember that being undone in light of God's goodness is the right place to start.

IF YOU'RE TOO UNDONE

Maybe that's not you though. Maybe you feel a bit too undone. I think a lot of Christ followers get stuck in the undone place. Sometimes we catch a glimpse of the train of God's robe and the depth of our sin, and we are crushed by how ridiculously we fall short. We fail to move on to the hopeful humility that flows from God's forgiveness.

If you've got the undone part down already, I want this Bible study to help you move beyond the shame of your sin to the joy-inducing, peace-producing thrill that comes from a lifestyle of repentance and a happy relationship with Jesus.

We were made to live in the light, confessing and repenting and renouncing our shame, because Jesus was shamed in our place. You can have that.

So, let's do this. Join me in Scripture for the next few weeks, and let's see the freedom available to us when we deeply experience the mercy of God. Let's study the Bible, do what it says, and enjoy what it gives.

I used to live life, doing my best, hoping and straining for wholeness and peace and perfection. I wanted so much to move past my mistakes and never again put my foot in my mouth. I longed for the day when Jesus would come through the clouds and fix me so that I wouldn't break anything else. I worked, hoped, and longed, without realizing that peace with God and joy in Jesus could exist for me today. Like, before I get off this airplane to go speak at this conference, I can be at peace. I can be shame-free. I can rest. Because this day, this weekend, this life, is not about how well I'm able to perform. It is always only about how Jesus performed in my place.

When I remember the good news of the gospel of Jesus, I remember that I can walk off this airplane not super perfect and polished, but rather, simply delighting in the truth and power of God's Word. Shame is a lie. Jesus is better. Let's discover this together.

WATCH

Write down any thoughts, verses, or things you want to remember as you watch the video for Session One.

DISCUSS

Fear and shame make people run away and hide. That's sort of the exact opposite thing as going to a small group, so I hope you won't run. I want you to stay. Quickly, let's think about what we just saw in Genesis 3—Adam and Eve and the beginning of shame.

***READ GENESIS 3:8-11*, as a group, keeping in mind that this is after Adam and Eve, the first two created people, sinned against God, doing the one thing He had commanded them not to do. What did they do when they heard God coming?**

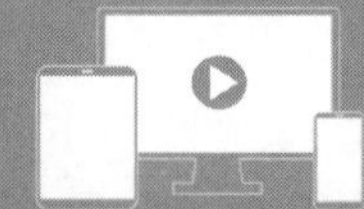

To access the video teaching sessions, use the instructions in the back of your Bible study book.

In verse 10, what does Adam tell God he was feeling?

Adam was afraid because he felt exposed. Embarrassed, he wanted to run. Every single one of you, and everyone you know, and all of their aunts, uncles, and dental hygienists know this feeling well. When others see our shame, we want to hide. Don't feel like joining this group for six weeks is a commitment to spill your guts and compound your shame. This next six weeks is not about your past or exposing your guilt for all to see. It's about God and what He's done to free you from it. Stay, focus on Him, and share what you're comfortable sharing. The more this group helps you see the power and love of God, the more you will want to run to Him, not run and hide.

Get to know your group! Share names, jobs, hobbies.

Do you have a childhood memory of your first moment of shame or embarrassment? Share it if you're brave.

Do you feel like you've had an "undone" moment, like Isaiah? If so, discuss what it was like when you recognized your need for God.

Have you ever felt stuck in your shame? What are some unhelpful (or only temporarily helpful) things you've turned to in those moments that didn't end up helping the way you hoped they would?

What hopes do you have in your personal walk with God as you enter into this study?

PRAY

Take time to come before God together and ask that He help each of you to understand His grace more deeply as you study and to extend that grace to one another.

LEADING A GROUP?
A free leader guide PDF is available for download at **lifeway.com/ashamed**

NOTES

NOTES

SESSION TWO

ASHAMED ISAIAH

JESUS REMOVES OUR SHAME

MEMORY VERSE

HE TOUCHED MY MOUTH WITH IT AND SAID: NOW THAT THIS HAS TOUCHED YOUR LIPS, **YOUR INIQUITY IS REMOVED AND YOUR SIN IS ATONED FOR.** THEN I HEARD THE VOICE OF THE LORD ASKING: WHO WILL I SEND? WHO WILL GO FOR US? I SAID: **HERE I AM. SEND ME.**

ISAIAH 6:7–8

(EMPHASIS ADDED)

DAY ONE

ASPIRING WITNESS PROTECTION PARTICIPANT

Isaiah 6

Every time I experience any conflict of any kind, I tell my husband to rent a moving truck and get ready to disconnect our power and water and move to a new city. I love getting away from problems. I have often wondered what it would take to join the Witness Protection Program but not because of any personal danger. I can't recall witnessing any substantive crimes. I just rrreaalllly like fresh starts.

MAN, I love fresh starts. I joke, but my life history, and the number of houses I've lived in, prove that there is a whole lot of truth in that joke.

I've been fresh-starting like it was my job since I was born, before I even had a say in it. By the age of five, I'd already lived in Los Angeles, NYC, Connecticut, and Miami. Since then, I've lived in Nashville and Orange County, and now Nashville again. Tallying up the number of addresses I've racked up since getting married sixteen years ago—oh my goodness. The answer is eleven. Just the other day, I was on the phone scheduling doctor appointments, and when they asked me for my zip code, I gave them a combination of my Tennessee zip and my most recent California zip.

I have had eleven home addresses in sixteen years. That's a whole lot of fresh starts. I guess I've informally and accidentally been witness-protectioning myself for the entirety of my adult life.

And I think I've sometimes been running from shame. I seem to lean toward running and hiding rather than staying and serving because I don't want to feel the shame of my brokenness or weakness. I don't want to be confronted with my depravity. It sounds awful, you know? I'd rather pack.

Can you relate? What is your typical response to conflict?

But God does incredible, miraculous, shame-crushing, joy-inducing things when we admit and confess our sin. One of the most beautiful examples of this is in the book of Isaiah.

READ ISAIAH 6. **Then look back at verses 1-5, and list five things Isaiah witnessed in those verses.**

1.

2.

3.

4.

5.

In the space below, write down the phrase that the seraphim were shouting to each other.

What a scene. It sounds terrifying, overwhelming, otherworldly—*kind of weird, actually*—right?

Now, let's look back at verses 6 and 7. A hot coal being put on a guy's mouth by an angel? Strange. But, what spiritual reality was happening during that physical act?

Isaiah's iniquity was removed. In the original Hebrew language, that the book of Isaiah was written in, the words *and your iniquity* are translated from a Hebrew word which means, *guilt, punishment for iniquity.*[1]

So, not only is Isaiah relieved of the punishment he's due, but he's also relieved of the guilt. That's huge. Consider that again—God doesn't just remove the punishment; He removes the guilt. We've all felt guilt before, so we know guilt is a too-heavy-to-carry punishment in itself.

Just like that—*poof*—guilt is removed. When you were a kid, did you ever face trouble and get let off the hook?

Get that circumstance in your mind. Did you get away with something? Maybe your parents still don't know about that lie or that night or that mistake to this day. Maybe you carried shame for a long time but eventually got over it. Or maybe you're still not over it.

Here, with the angels and God and Isaiah, we see a man who is thoroughly guilty standing before the God who sees all and knows all. And instead of destroying him, God forgives him. It's hard to even imagine what that must be like, right?

***READ ISAIAH 6:8-13*, and answer the following questions.**

What did God ask?

How did Isaiah answer?

What was the mission God had for Isaiah?

That mission sounds pretty horrible. Because not only was Isaiah being sent to deliver bad news from God, but God told Him how it was going to work out, and how it worked out was not great.

Has God ever called you to something that felt pretty horrible? Write about it below.

If you walked in obedience to that call, how did it work out for you and the people you were serving?

In those early figuring-it-out years of my faith, I wouldn't have had much to write in spaces like the one above. My fear and shame kept me from obedience. My fear and shame kept me from living for God, listening to God, and being blessed by taking part in the mission of God.

But the more I began to understand my own sinfulness and just how much it took for God to redeem me—just how much love and mercy was involved—the easier it was to take baby steps in the direction He led. As soon as I started taking those steps, the blessings He poured out on me and my family were overwhelming.

Blessings like purpose, peace, and joy.

Do fear and shame keep you from walking in obedience? If so, what does that look like in your life?

If you answered yes to that last question, remember what Isaiah's coal-meets-lips scenario means for you. Like Isaiah, we are unworthy when faced with the purity of our perfect, all-powerful God. But that hot coal reminds us that God is so loving that He offers us forgiveness. While Isaiah's forgiveness was symbolized with a burning coal, our forgiveness is offered through the sacrificial death and resurrection of Jesus Christ.

What baby step can you take as you seek to live the mission God is calling you to? How can you say, "Here I am; send me," this week?

I think Andrew Davis sums this up powerfully. In *Exalting Jesus in Isaiah*, he writes:

> *What a beautiful sequence in this narrative: a vision of the enthroned Lord in his glory leads to overpowering heavenly worship, and it also leads to Isaiah's awareness of his sinfulness, which leads to him crying out against himself, which leads to the atoning work for his sin, which leads to hearing the Lord call for a messenger, which leads to Isaiah presenting himself for service. In this sense, Isaiah 6 stands as a lasting paradigm for all who would enter the Lord's service.*[2]

In short, awareness and repentance of sin leads us to offer ourselves up to the Lord for His work.

Close out this day meditating on this beautiful paradigm and praying that the Lord will help your mind release the shame of your failures, that He'll help you remember His Son's payment for your sins, that He'll help you renounce your fear of the future, and that you'll feel His nearness as you do something eternal today.

DAY TWO

COWERING FROM CONSECRATED COUSINS

Luke 14:7–14,25–33; Isaiah 6:7

The times I've felt most ashamed happen to have been the same times I was witnessing someone else's apparent act of altruism or sacrifice. Someone else's "Here I am; send me" moments often point out my lack of them.

Before we started the process of adopting our middle daughter from China, I will never forget running into some distant cousins at a family function and avoiding them like I avoided germs in 2020. Note: They are lovely cousins, but the thing is, they were fresh off the heels of two international adoptions for a couple of sweetheart girls with special needs.

How wonderful, beautiful, and noble, right?

Well, rather than asking questions or commending their beautiful family or offering to help hold a baby so the mom could make herself a plate, I had this weirdly timed urge to go stand in the bathroom and check my hair really quick. Coincidentally, that happened every time they came near.

In my mind, the adoption-loving cousins were in the throne room with the shouting seraphim, and I was unworthy and unwilling—the opposite of all the good things they were.

Their selflessness shined an incriminating spotlight on how selfishly I was living.

Their courage reminded me of how comfortable I'd become hiding from my purpose in the world.

Enter the restroom. Check hair. Feel shame. Repeat.

Their evident fruit reminded me of how fruitless my life looked. And I didn't like it.

Woe is me! I am unworthy of having small talk with these superhero humans, and I'm not sure I want to do what it seems to take to be worthy.

Though my comfort-craving heart lies to me and tells me that a good life is an easy one, God has never skirted around the reality of His own holiness, and the very legitimate cost of being one of His followers.

Can you think of a time in your own life that being around holiness or goodness shined a light on your guilt and made you want to run away? Reflect on that in the space below.

READ LUKE 14:7-14.

In this passage of Scripture, Jesus was eating at the house of one of the leading Pharisees, a religious leader of the time. After observing their behavior, He taught them about humility.

How would you define *humility*?

How is humility demonstrated in this example from Jesus?

The Bible talks about humility a lot. We must humble ourselves to know God. We must humble ourselves to recognize our need for Him in the first place.

READ LUKE 14:25-33. **What is the cost of following Jesus?**

Why do you think this teaching came after a teaching on humility?

The cost of following Christ is great. We must be willing to bear our own crosses—ready to give up everything to follow Him. This is including, but not limited to, giving up our pride. When we recognize our need for Jesus, when we realize we can't save ourselves or earn holiness, when we understand we will never be worthy on our own, that is humbling.

It might even sound humiliating. Well, one of the coolest things I ever learned was about how different "humility" and "humiliation" are.

Here are some synonyms for the word *humiliate*: dishonor, disgrace, mortify, shame, degrade, abase, debase.

On the contrary, here's a list of synonyms for *humility*: modesty, meekness, lack of pride, lowliness.

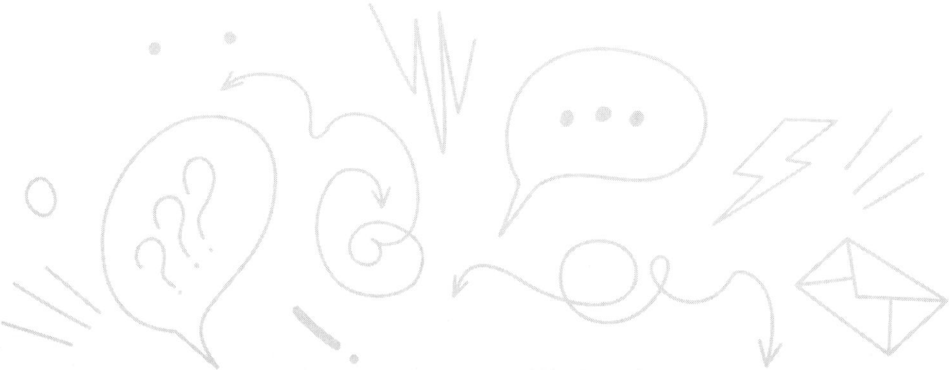

Those are pretty different lists for two words that sound so similar and are so often mixed up.

One word suggests a sort of self-loathing, and the other looks a lot like Jesus.

Do you struggle with equating the two? Do you feel holier when you are beating yourself up? Take a minute to write out what this struggle looks like (or has looked like in the past) in your personal life.

In the table below, write down what God's Word says about true biblical humility.

SCRIPTURE	WHAT WE LEARN ABOUT HUMILITY
Micah 6:8	
Proverbs 18:12	
Isaiah 57:15	
1 Peter 5:5	

Whew. The Bible has a lot to say about humility, doesn't it? And that list is nowhere near exhaustive. Looking over all this Scripture, one thing I noticed is how frequently God's people are commanded to be humble.

Commands like these can be hard to wrap your mind around, because with any fruit of the Spirit or Christlike way of being, if you pursue said good thing for the wrong reasons, you never find it. Like, if I say to myself, *I WANT TO BE HUMBLE SO THAT I AM AWESOME AND APPLAUDED BY GOD AND PEOPLE*, I'm doing it wrong.

> ***LOOK BACK AT ISAIAH 6:7.*** **What was it that caused Isaiah's humility?**

Forgiveness! Isaiah's experience and awareness of the undeserved and dramatic forgiveness he received from the holy, perfect, true God is what humbled him.

> *As you close out this day, ask the Holy Spirit to help you identify where you might be stuck in humiliation. Ask Him to help your heart move toward humility.*

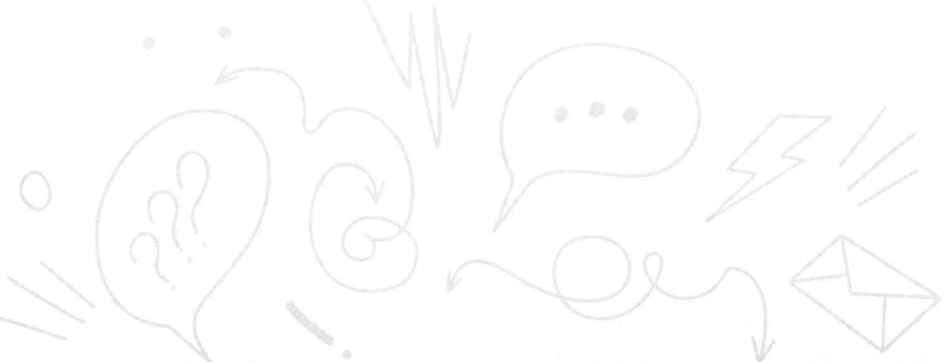

DAY THREE

A SWEET, SHAMELESS REDHEAD

Isaiah 50; Luke 7:36–50; Psalm 103:11–14

Isaiah 50 is about listening to God. Listening to God, even when it means suffering. After His encounter with God in chapter 6, Isaiah was a willing prophet who obediently delivered tons of bad news about God's coming judgment. Isaiah listened and obeyed. Good job, Isaiah! But remember, Isaiah was also "a man of unclean lips." Isaiah was a sinner.

Other than being the bearer of bad news, Isaiah is known for prophesying about the coming Messiah. If you're new to Christianity, and you don't know what any of those words mean, prophesying, in this context, means foretelling the future. "Messiah" means "Savior." Isaiah was, yes, telling the nation of Judah a whole lot about God's coming judgment, but he was also sharing the ground-breaking, globe-shaking news that God, in His mercy, was going to send a Savior (Jesus)—the One who would, quoting the *Lord of the Rings* series here, "make everything sad come untrue."[3]

And here, in Isaiah 50, we get to hear more from Isaiah, a sometimes obedient, but flawed and imperfect servant, writing about the coming of a perfectly obedient, perfectly unselfish Servant. He was writing about Jesus before Jesus came.

LOOK UP ISAIAH 50, AND READ VERSES 4-10 **from the perspective of the perfectly obedient Servant to come (Jesus). What does verse 4 say God has given Him?**

What does Jesus say He did not do, in verse 5?

What future thing does it sound like Jesus is describing in verse 6? (Hint: read John 19)

I want you to pay such special attention to Isaiah 50:7. So, go ahead and copy it down in the space below.

In this verse, we can see the nature of Jesus displayed—He is one hundred percent man, but He is also one hundred percent God. The math doesn't add up, but it's true. He is the Son of God, sent to live a sinless life on earth by the Father, to die on the cross for our sins, and to be raised again, defeating death.

For most of us humans, the events described by Isaiah in verse 6 would be humiliating. To be beaten and mocked and spit upon? Can you think of anything more humiliating?

However, verse 7 tells us Jesus will not be humiliated. Why? Because He is God, and He knows the end. He knows the results will not be humiliation but vindication.

Because of this heaven-touching-earth moment, we can echo our Savior and say, "I have not been humiliated . . . I will not be put to shame." That is true for us in Jesus. Hallelujah.

So, what can our lives look like when we remember and embrace this reality?

I used to work at a church in my twenties. This was before I'd spent much time with Jesus or much time in His Word, and I remember the sweet redhead who worked at the front desk just exploding with love and happiness. She was truly the quintessential front desk person as she made everyone who came to her feel completely grenaded with care and kindness. I remember commenting on it one day and she said, "Oh, the one who's been forgiven much loves much!"

How brilliant! I thought, not realizing that she was literally quoting Jesus.

READ LUKE 7:36-50. **How did the woman in this story behave around Jesus, and what did the Pharisees think about it?**

In verses 44-47, Jesus explains why her behavior was appropriate and beautiful. Put His explanation into your own words in the space below.

Is there someone you have encountered in your life who possessed what looked like genuine humility? Describe how that person lived and how they made you feel.

What a beautiful thing that the Spirit of God in the lives of believers leads to humility. But, people, even the ones who look a lot like Jesus, will let us down in this life. Thankfully, we can study the life of Jesus, and in Him, we see and know and hear from the only One who perfectly humbled Himself (Phil. 2:8) even though He had every reason not to.

In seasons when I've suffered with depression or grief or anxiety, when I've spent hours awake in the middle of the night cycling through the worst moments on my "shame reel" (more on the shame reel later), the thought of being someone like Sweet Redhead feels impossible.

In the space below, quickly jot down the mindsets or negative thoughts you carry with you.

READ PSALM 103:11-14. **What point is the psalmist making about our sins (or transgressions)?**

What point is he making about God?

Okay, spend more time on this part please. ☺

Go back over the list you wrote on the previous page of your negative thoughts and scribble out those things with passion and pressure like your life depends on it, so you can't make out a single word you wrote.

Jesus is better and stronger than anything you can ever write. He is and gives His best and His strength to you. Because of Jesus's sacrifice, our compassionate God has removed our transgressions "as far as the east is from the west."

Now, close off this day, and take all the time you need, to write down as many things as you can think of that remind you of the goodness of God. When you are tempted to replay your shame reel or tell yourself lies about who God is and who you are, remember what the Bible says—our God is good and compassionate. Use the following verses to jog your memory and write down ways that you've noticed this goodness in your own life.

- Exodus 34:6
- Psalm 23
- Psalm 145:8-10
- John 3:15-18
- Philippians 1:6
- James 1:17

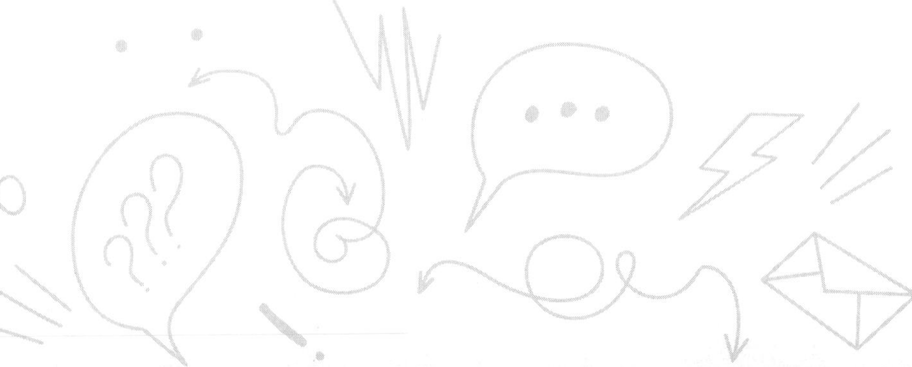

DAY FOUR

BROKEN CARS AND iPAD DEBTORS

Isaiah 53:1–12

When I was a poor newlywed, I worked at a school and shared a car with my pastor-husband who worked about thirty minutes from my job. I often had to carpool or wait for rides. One day, the kindergarten teacher at my school noticed my plight and said, "I have an extra car sitting in my garage that's not being driven. My husband and I want to loan it to you."

What a gift! I was so grateful. Married life with two cars? What would that even be like?

But almost immediately, car-borrowing-tragedy struck. The loaner was an older convertible Mazda®, and one day, I rolled down the window to find that it wouldn't roll back up. I parked the car in front of our little shack. (Our first "house" is what we now affectionately refer to as "The Shack." You can read more about this delightful home in Chapter Two: Worst Poor Person of my book, *You're the Worst Person in the World.*)

Anyway, I parked in front of The Shack in a panic, as a few rain droplets threatened the interior leather of my borrowed car. The next few moments are a blur. We had no garage and no way to shield the car from the elements, so I ran inside and found black trash bags and duct tape (things you always keep on hand when you're broke), and I duct taped the sweet kindergarten teacher's car up.

It was so horrifying and humiliating having to tell her that we broke her car. We ordered the broken window part but couldn't afford to have it put back together. I told her we were working on it, and in an act of sheer mercy, she said, "Scarlet, don't worry about it. We will fix the window. Just leave it in the parking lot."

Humiliating, yes. Relieving? So much yes.

Have you ever had someone take the fall for you? Someone pay your debt? Write about it below.

Fast forward a decade, and we found ourselves in a new city with new jobs, two fully functioning cars and enough extra income to buy an iPad® but not enough to be able to replace it if something were to happen.

A family from our church with a bunch of young kids had my husband's iPad, and when I went to pick it up at their house, the mom approached me with shame in her eyes and a hilarious sentence to share. "My son threw your iPad against the tree. I'm so sorry."

She handed me the rectangle of broken glass and I said, "Don't worry about it."

And it was easy to say that. Not because we had money to replace it, but because people had done the same for us. God had done the same for us.

When you personally know how it feels to have a debt paid, it's a joy to do the same for others.

When I think of that family and the broken iPad, I'm so grateful we were able to treat them the way the kindergarten teacher treated me.

It should work the same way for us as followers of Christ.

We can have the joy of living out each day we're given in light of this overwhelming debt we've been relieved of. We can be the most gracious people in the world because we know what it is to be ashamed and humiliated and panicked because we've broken something and don't have the means to fix it.

READ ISAIAH 53:1-12. **Who is this "guilt offering" that Isaiah is writing about, and what does this passage tell you about Him?**

It's amazing to me, the detail we are given about Jesus hundreds of years before His birth. God's people were told what He'd be like, how He'd arrive, and about the shame He would carry.

LOOK BACK AT ISAIAH 53. **What does verse 6 say about us?**

How did God respond to our actions, according to that verse?

Look up the following verses, and write down what they say about our debt.

SCRIPTURE	WHAT WE LEARN ABOUT DEBT
Romans 6:23	
Ephesians 1:7	
Hebrews 7:27	
1 Peter 1:18-19	
1 Peter 2:24	
1 John 2:1-2	

We are so indebted to our Creator and Rescuer, it would break our brains to fully grasp it. A. W. Tozer has much more eloquent language than "break our brains" to explain how very different, holy, and high God is, and how very needy, poor, and dependent we are.

He wrote, "We must not think of God as the highest in an ascending order of beings, starting with the single cell and going on up from the fish to the bird to the animal to man to angel to cherub to God . . . He is as high above an archangel as above a caterpillar, for the gulf that separates the archangel from the caterpillar is but finite, while the gulf between God and the archangel is infinite."[4]

Spend a few moments praying, thanking God for sending His Son to die in your place. Thank Him for His forgiveness and love.

DAY FIVE

ISAIAH ALL OVER THE PLACE

John 12:37–41; Luke 4:16–19; Isaiah 61:1–2

The book of Isaiah is the most frequently quoted book elsewhere in the Bible. Why? Why is it so important that other biblical authors kept sharing it? What about Isaiah is so fundamental to our faith?

Well, put simply, Isaiah kept saying that Jesus was coming. Guys, Isaiah clearly presented the message of the gospel seven hundred years before the gospel was fulfilled. He predicted it in great detail—detail that turned out to be completely, hair-splittingly accurate.

I just watched *The Gray Man* on Netflix twice in a week. It's rare that my husband can talk me into a "boy movie," but if there's some sort of heartwarming love thread, I can look past the dark weapon-y stuff and get sucked in.

In short, the movie was about a CIA guy (Ryan Gosling) and a bunch of bad guys trying to kill him. My favorite relationship in the movie was the big bro/little sis dynamic between Gosling and a tweenaged girl with a heart condition that he was looking after.

I think I loved the movie so much because of his relationship with this girl who had a heart problem. She was kidnapped and leveraged, and he always showed up. He'd wink at her and then take out a bunch of bad guys for her. "Just another Thursday," he said.

Doesn't that do something to you? Don't you want to believe that your Rescuer is going to pluck you out of all the pain? Don't you feel to the depths that you're a little girl with a heart condition, and Jesus is fighting the world to save you?

It feels too good to be true now, so can you even imagine the hearers of Isaiah's words back in those days—those pre-Rescuer days?

All this to say, the book of Isaiah is important and massively quoted because it pointed to the reality of the Rescuer who was to come. And then He came, and He and the people around Him were like, "Remember what Isaiah said? Open your eyes!"

OPEN UP TO JOHN 12:37-41. **In my Bible, there's a subheading that says, "Isaiah's Prophecies Fulfilled." Read through the verses, and in the space below, write down the verses from Isaiah referenced in this passage in John. (Hint: look at the footnotes or cross references in your Bible.)**

Rewrite the prophecies from Isaiah in your own words.

It's hard to really capture the significance by pulling little pieces of Scripture out like this, so if you have the time today, I'd really encourage you to flip back, even if it's just to the beginning of John chapter 12.

Right there at the beginning, we're reminded that Jesus just raised Lazarus from the dead. The Gospels are so incredible. Miracle after miracle is performed. And in John 12, we see Jesus's triumphal entry, where He rides a young donkey to fulfill a prophecy from Zechariah 9:9. Even the words the people are shouting at Him are quoted from Psalm 118:25-26. It's amazing.

So here in John, we see Jesus in real time living out the calling that Isaiah prophesied about all the way down to the state of the hearts and ears and eyes of the people He was around.

READ LUKE 4:16-19. **What town was Jesus in, and what did He read from?**

What Jesus read there in His hometown was not random, at all.

READ ISAIAH 61:1-2. **Which specific phrases do you see here that you just read in the gospel of Luke?**

Isn't that incredible? And it's just one of many examples of this. Jesus was the long-awaited hope, the way-better-than-Ryan-Gosling Hero. He didn't provide temporary safety to a girl with a heart condition. He bled and died and rose again, giving eternal hope to our broken hearts.

Raise your hand if you forgot you were doing a Bible study about shame? Looking at intricate fulfillments of this hope makes it hard to think about lesser things—even our own shame. And that's the whole point.

God is so wonderful, so compassionate, so loving. He overwhelms lesser things in our lives and gives us what we need. He has given us signs and wonders and details and miracles—as if salvation wasn't enough! We can look through this alive and active book (Heb. 4:12) and see His provision and His hand, throughout history, on every page. Why do we so often doubt His hand in our own lives?

This may look a little daunting, but it's going to be really cool. On the left, you'll see a New Testament reference and what the reference is referring to. Pretend you're in school, and being the very scholarly person you are, as you read these passages, pay very close attention to the little letters, numbers, and footnotes. In each of these verses, you can see which verse of prophecy it is fulfilling and where that's found in Isaiah. And by the way, this is just the smallest sampling of examples. There are so many more, it's absurd. I'll do the first couple for you. Okay, here we go.

MATTHEW 1:23 – A virgin will become pregnant	*Isaiah 7:14*
MATTHEW 12:21 – Jesus is hope for the Gentiles	*Isaiah 42:1-4*
MARK 9:48 – What eternal separation from God is like ("Fire is not quenched . . . ")	
LUKE 4:17–19 – Jesus is anointed to preach	
JOHN 12:39–40 – Blinded eyes and hardened hearts	
ACTS 8:32–33 – Jesus led like a sheep to the slaughter	
ROMANS 9:33 – Believers will not be disappointed	
1 CORINTHIANS 15:54–56 – Death swallowed up	

Okay. No shame to the homework slackers, but if you didn't look up all those passages, just look at that very last one. I'll even put some of it here in the book for you.

> *. . . then the saying that is written will take place: Death has been swallowed up in victory. Where, death, is your victory? Where, death, is your sting? The sting of death is sin, and the power of sin is the law. But thanks be to God, who gives us the victory through our Lord Jesus Christ!*
>
> **1 CORINTHIANS 15:54-56**

And the call back in Isaiah 25:8: "He will destroy death forever."

What better news do we have than that? Jesus is good news. The gospel is good news. Death has been "swallowed up in victory." Your shame from failures—past, present, and future—shrivel up in that kind of hope, right? How should you close off this day? Believe it. Memorize it. Cling to it. Jesus has swallowed up our shame and given us the victory. Take the day off, Ryan Gosling. We can have true and lasting peace.

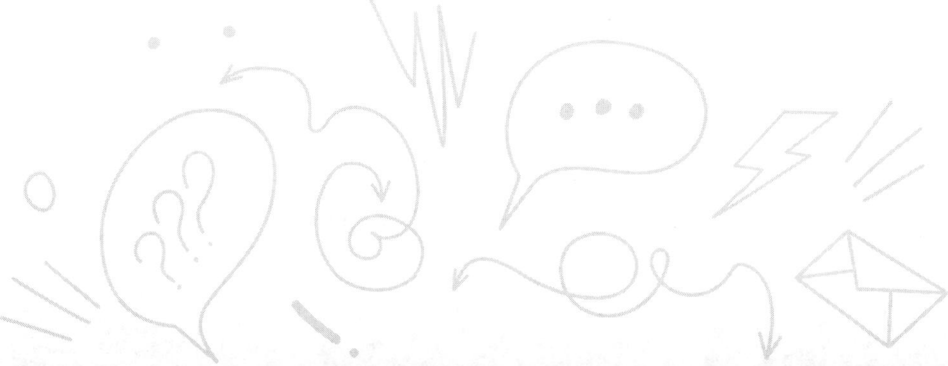

WATCH

Write down any thoughts, verses, or things you want to remember as you watch the video for Session Two.

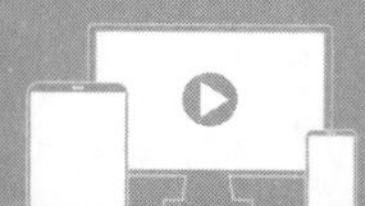

To access the video teaching sessions, use the instructions in the back of your Bible study book.

WATCH

Write down any thoughts, verses, or things you want to remember as you watch the video for Session Two.

DISCUSS

On Day One, we read about when Isaiah was forgiven in the throne room of God. Have you ever experienced awe and undoneness over the holiness of God? How so?

This session's main idea is "Jesus removes our shame." If you are open to sharing, tell your group a brief testimony of shame you carried and how the Lord is helping you release it.

In the chart you filled out on Day Four (p. 36), which verse about debt was most meaningful to you? Why?

What is one new habit you can add to your life to help you fight shame with God's Word?

PRAY

Thank God for sending Jesus to make a way for sinful people to be near to a holy God. Spend the remainder of your time in prayer. Pray specifically that God would help you and each member of your group fight feelings of shame and guilt by filling your minds with the truth of His Word.

FROM THIS WEEK'S STUDY

Review this week's memory verse.

He touched my mouth with it and said: Now that this has touched your lips, your iniquity is removed and your sin is atoned for. Then I heard the voice of the Lord asking: Who should I send? Who will go for us? I said: Here I am. Send me.

ISAIAH 6:7-8

LEADING A GROUP?

A free leader guide PDF is available for download at **lifeway.com/ashamed**

SESSION THREE

ASHAMED AT THE WELL

JESUS GIVES LIVING WATER TO THIRSTY HEARTS

MEMORY VERSE

JESUS SAID, "EVERYONE WHO DRINKS FROM THIS WATER WILL GET THIRSTY AGAIN. **BUT WHOEVER DRINKS FROM THE WATER THAT I WILL GIVE HIM WILL NEVER GET THIRSTY AGAIN.** IN FACT, THE WATER I WILL GIVE HIM WILL BECOME A WELL OF WATER SPRINGING UP IN HIM FOR ETERNAL LIFE."

JOHN 4:13–14

(EMPHASIS ADDED)

DAY ONE

AM I GETTING MUGGED OR MEAL-TRAINED?

John 4:1–14; 7:37–38; 10:10

Have you ever been shocked by someone's kindness? I grew up in big cities—LA, NYC, and Miami. I didn't get a taste of southern hospitality until I moved to Nashville as an adult. In big cities, you walk fast, do your thing, and watch out for yourself. But I'll never forget my first day in Nashville when a man in a parking lot said, "Hey!," and I jumped in fear, assuming I was about to die. But he wasn't a murderer or a mugger. He was just saying hello.

In Nashville, people brought me meals when I had babies and waved me ahead to go first at four-way stops. It was weird and striking, experiencing such a gracious cultural context. But meal trains and cordial drivers aren't a huge deal compared to the text we're about to look at.

Today's story isn't "city girl meets southerners." That's because Jews and Samaritans were not just slightly culturally different. They did not mix at all. They hated each other.

Samaria had been captured by the Assyrians, who deported many of the Jews, settling with and marrying remaining Jews and practicing their religion their way. So, Jewish people looked down on Samaritans politically, religiously, and racially. D. A. Carson explains the feeling that the Jews "viewed the Samaritans not only as the children of political rebels, but as racial half-breeds whose religion was tainted by various unacceptable elements."[1]

Their beef also included a disagreement about where they believed God's people should worship.

The conflict was so intense by the time Jesus was around, that Jews wouldn't even pass through Samaria when they traveled. They'd cross the Jordan River instead. This wasn't bumping into a frenemy at the grocery store. This was Capulet and Montegue type tension.

There was then a unique sort of cultural shame that this woman likely felt before Jesus even opened His mouth, just at the sight of a Jewish man at a Samaritan well. So, when Jesus spoke to the woman at the well, it wasn't just a friendly Nashville wave hello. It was a radical, beautiful, cross-cultural, theological statement.

What kinds of cultural shame exist in our world today?

READ JOHN 4:1-14. **Why did Jesus stop in Samaria when He was traveling through?**

What did He ask of the Samaritan woman and how did she react?

Have you ever questioned someone's kindness as too good to be true? The example I immediately think of is when a child wants five dollars or a Sonic® slush or a day off school, so they clean the dishes and approach with a hug and a, "Mom, you're SO beautiful and wonderful and I love you!" Mom responds, "Okay, what do you want?"

Think of a time you've questioned someone's motives. Jot down a few of the details.

Did your assumption of their motive turn out to be true or false?

The Samaritan woman knew it didn't make sense for a Jew to stop by for some water, so she questioned Him. What's this guy's angle?

What did Jesus tell her He could offer her in verse 10?

How did she show she didn't understand what He meant?

I'm going to be honest with you—if I didn't already know this story, I, too, would question the phrase "living water." What does that mean? I picture some sort of sci-fi water creature made with CGI. But Jesus often used words with double meanings. Later in the Gospel, He explains a little more.

READ JOHN 7:37-38. **What is the living water in this passage?**

"If you knew," Jesus said, "you would ask him . . . " (4:10). That is such a powerful statement. Not just for the woman at the well, who clearly didn't know who she was talking to, but for long-time believers like me, who walk around with shame, forgetting that I have all-the-time access to the One who died to take that shame away. "If you only knew . . . "

FLIP FORWARD A FEW PAGES TO JOHN 10:10. **Why did Jesus come to earth?**

We who do know Christ should ask Him for help when we feel ashamed. We ask even if we are ashamed because of religious, cultural, or racial tension like the Samaritan woman. These things feel too big to tackle, but just like Jesus walked right into Samaria and spoke right to that woman, He walked right into our broken world and offered us an abundant life to live.

The living water is available if we will drink, no matter the severity of the source of our shame. Shame is washed away when we know Jesus. When we ask, He gives living water.

> *Today, pray about and around the sort of shame you or people you interact with might experience, not based on sin, but based on outside expectations. Pray that you and those you minister to will experience healing and renewed confidence, the kind that comes from the Lord.*

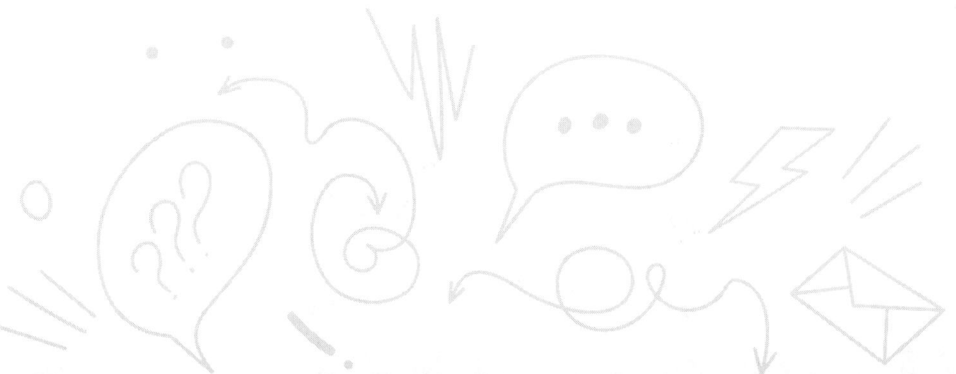

DAY TWO

RECOGNIZED AT THE REGISTER

John 4:11–26

I had an unusual childhood. You don't recognize you lived an unusual childhood until you're an adult and enough people say, "That's not normal." My mom was a literal TV and movie star and my biological dad was a magician/fire-eater. What a sentence. But it was totally normal to me.

Everywhere we went, no matter the city or store, my mom would get stopped. People would freak out, ask for her autograph, the whole thing. My mom has a very distinct, high-pitched voice, and oftentimes, rather than people recognizing her right away they'd say things like, "You sound JUST LIKE that girl from *Saturday Night Live*." (That's the show she was on.)

I remember her sweetly smiling and saying, "I'm her," and sometimes the person wouldn't believe it. We'd leave the store or the restaurant or the city with that person having no idea who they just met. I'd seen enough people freak out over meeting her, that I remember in those moments thinking, "This person has no idea who they're talking to! If they believed her, this would be a highlight of their year, and they'd talk about it forever!"

Jesus wasn't a sparkly TV star, but word of His miraculous healings and His fulfillment prophecy was spreading. People who recognized who He really was walked away with changed lives. But many people didn't believe. Many people didn't know. They walked away not recognizing the magnitude of the Person they'd met.

At first, the woman at the well clearly didn't understand who she was talking to either.

> ***READ JOHN 4:11-26.*** **What questions did the woman ask Jesus in verses 11 and 12?**

I love this. I love how her questions reveal her lack of understanding and I love how Jesus, as He often did, responded, not with an answer to her question, but with what she needed to actually understand.

I can think back on so many times I've prayed, asking God questions about details and specifics—temporary things—and He has answered me by lifting my eyes upward, by expanding my view, and by reminding me of who He is and what is eternal.

Write briefly about a time in your life you did not understand.

How would your feelings have changed if you had been reminded of who God is—faithful, good, compassionate, sovereign—in your moment of confusion?

Something else I appreciate about today's passage is that it's a comfort for those of us who open our Bibles and don't always understand what we're looking at. We might open the Bible trying to find answers or fixes. Sometimes we might read for answers to questions like, "God, when will my job/boss/work situation change?" Or "God, how long will I have to wait for these medical results?" And instead of Magic 8 Ball® answers, we're met with Jesus. Instead of logistics, we find love, comfort, and peace in the living, active Word.

Do you ever ask God questions or look to His Word for the wrong reasons? What does that look like for you?

LOOK BACK AT VERSES 13-14. **What does the living water Jesus offers do for people?**

"Eternal life" can sound like a weird phrase, and we can sometimes get desensitized to it, but it is the ultimate good thing. Read it again: *eternal life.* The absence of death, disease, and pain. The presence of God, glory, perfection. Never ending.

That's what Jesus was offering the Samaritan woman. It wasn't an extra special seltzer water. It was forever and abundant life that day.

So, where does shame come into play in this story? Let's take a look.

REREAD VERSES 15-26.

Notice how Jesus chose to reveal Himself to this woman. He could have told her about the living water, seen her lack of understanding, and went on His way. But He revealed Himself as more than an unlikely conversation partner by telling her about the shameful things He knew she'd done and was doing, things He shouldn't and couldn't have known about.

How would you have responded if a stranger listed out your areas of shame in a conversation?

How does the woman respond? Who does she think Jesus is at first?

In verse 26, Jesus is clearer than clear about who He is. He identifies Himself as the long-awaited Messiah. Here, our well woman has an opportunity to either believe Jesus is who He says He is and walk away changed or be like those cashiers with my mom—"You might sound like her, but you're not her. Next customer."

Jesus offered the woman a chance to believe, and in believing, a chance at freedom from shame. She was a shame-filled woman. He was a shame-lifting Savior. And in one well-side moment Jesus offered her the abundant life she would never be able to find on her own.

DAY THREE

BEFORE AND AFTER

John 4:27–42

It's such an amazing, beautiful, shame-slaying thing when people share their testimonies. The woman at the well had a lot to say in the "before" part of her testimony. But today, we get to see how God redeemed her "before" for a beautiful "after," not just for herself, but for those around her.

What adjectives would you use to describe the Samaritan woman's "before"?

READ JOHN 4:27-42. **How would you describe the Samaritan woman's "after"?**

Jesus told her He had living water. Then, when His disciples told Him to eat, He spoke of food.

What was Jesus communicating through His figurative use of food and water?

I'm currently obsessed with Chipotle® bowls and Arnold Palmers® (which is iced tea and lemonade). I don't know your go-tos, but I know you have them, because our core needs as human beings are food and drink. Without them, our bodies die. A relationship with God through Jesus is like that but on a forever level. If our bodies don't have food and water, they die. If our souls don't have Jesus, we are just marking days and walking in hopelessness. He is who we were made for, so there is no true life in His absence.

Do you think someone looking at your life would know that Jesus is necessary for your survival? Why or why not?

What can you do to demonstrate more clearly that Jesus is the reason for your hope?

Reading about this Samaritan woman is so encouraging, because shame-wise, she had so much going against her. She was carrying her shame for reasons that were her fault and reasons that were outside of her control. But after she had this encounter with Jesus, everything changed.

This woman's testimony was brief. Read it again in verse 39. What did she say, and how did people react?

What about the woman's testimony do you think compelled the people to find Jesus and learn more?

Verse 39 tells us that many Samaritans believed because of her testimony, but there were others who needed more. They went to Jesus Himself and then believed because of their own encounters with Him. Isn't that incredible? It's so true for all of us who follow Jesus. If we share our stories of how the Messiah moved us from shame and slavery and hopelessness to abundant life, we will get to see lives changed, for sure. But what that story-sharing is doing, mainly, is pointing people to Jesus and leading them to their own encounter with Him.

If you are a believer, how would you share about your encounter with Jesus in one line, like the woman at the well?

Have you ever gotten to lead someone to Jesus by sharing your story? Or have you ever heard someone else's story of their encounter with Jesus and been moved? What was it about their story that was compelling to you?

Write more about it below, and finish out this day by thanking Jesus for allowing us to help people walk away from shame and toward life in Jesus.

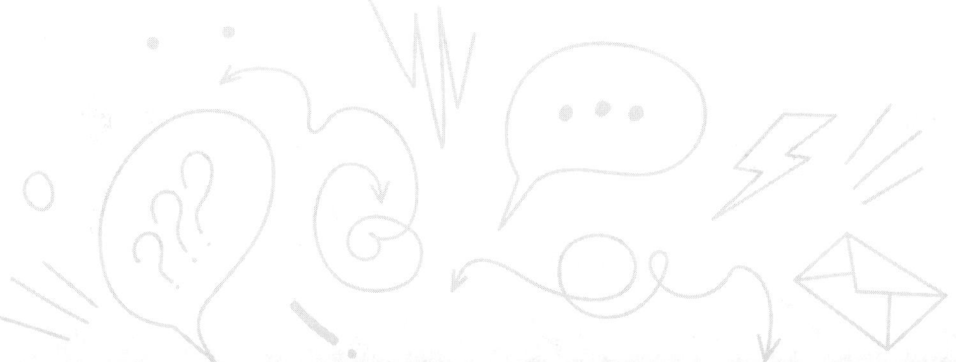

DAY FOUR

THE CYCLE OF SELF CARE

John 7:37–39

In today's look at chapter 7 of John, Jesus talked about living water again. Here's a little context. At this point, Jesus's ministry was still not public, but word about Him was spreading. The beginning of chapter 7 tells us that Jesus was traveling in Galilee because in Judea the Jewish religious people were trying to kill Him. To the Jewish people who had made their whole lives about following God's law, Jesus was a blasphemer, a threat to the system, and Someone acting as though He were God Himself (He is).

So, here in chapter 7, we see Jesus teaching at a festival. If you look back at the Old Testament laws, Jewish men had a number of feasts they were required to go to every year (Deut. 16). Based on the timeline, historians think the celebration Jesus was attending in John 7 was the Feast of Booths (or the Festival of Tabernacles). The event lasted seven days (Lev. 23), and it was a time when Jewish people would celebrate that God had brought the Israelites through the wilderness. So, Galilee would have been busy at this time of year. Lots of people around. Plenty of partying. But Jesus came secretly, still not broadcasting His presence because His time had "not yet arrived" (v. 6).

> ***READ JOHN 7:37-39.*** **What need do the people have that Jesus identifies here?**

Thirst for water is a universal need. Remember 2020, and how bizarre it was to see everyone scared and suffering over the same thing? Everyone was suffering; everyone felt their need. It's cool to me that Jesus spoke to people in a way that immediately cut through whatever social or cultural filters they had. Thirst. Need. We all have it. We all know what longing feels like. We all know what it is to want for something, to desire the always fleeting and ever-elusive feeling of being quenched. Just like the woman at the well, people knew that the comfort and provision they could find on their own wasn't everlasting.

What do you look to for comfort lately?

If you're honest, do you see that comfort-seeking as a desire to mask shame? How so?

If you look to the experts of our day, they'll tell you that "positive self talk" and "self care" is the answer to combatting your shame. But try those things for a while, and you'll end up returning to the well, again and again, longing for something that will heal you in a deeper way, longing for a comfort and satisfaction that goes the distance. You were made to hear another voice. You were made for a deeper care. And your Father wants you to have it.

What does Jesus tell the people here in Galilee they must do to quench their thirst?

What does verse 39 say He is referring to when He promises streams of living water?

For the hearers of those words in Galilee, Jesus was promising His Spirit to come. The God who made us promised to live in us. He was promising eternal healing from sin and the shame it brings.

As Jesus's hearers today, we have the privilege and thrill of knowing we can have access to that Spirit right now. This moment. Because Jesus is who He said He was and did what He said He'd do, we can be quenched. Our shame can be undone. Our thirst can be satisfied. "If anyone is thirsty, let him come to me and drink."

What does it mean to have streams of living water flowing in you? What feelings came to your mind as you read that?

It makes me feel hopeful, full, light, comforted. I don't have to go back to the "well" of myself, of the things I try to fill the void or cover my shame again and again and again and again. Instead, I have the answer. My shame doesn't have to be covered by me. I am filled with the Holy Spirit!

Close out today, praying and thanking God for His Spirit—the living water He gives us that is like a stream flowing from deep within us.

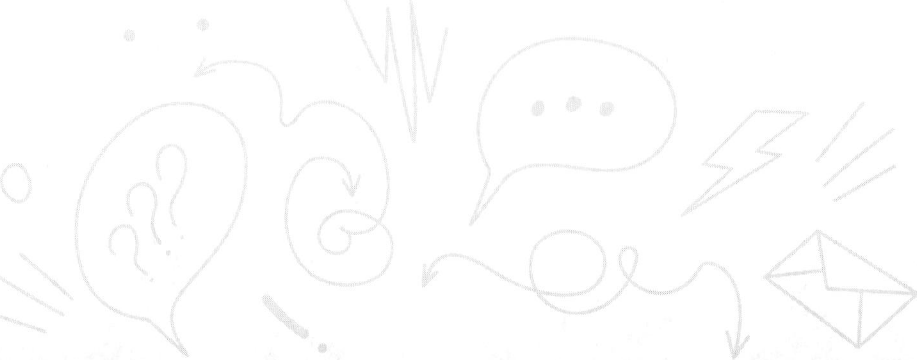

DAY FIVE

WHERE TO GO WHEN IT WON'T GO AWAY

Revelation 21:1–6

Every time I think I've just shared my favorite passage of Scripture with you, I get to the next one and I'm like, "OH, YEAH, NO! THIS IS THE BEST!"

Revelation 21 is a place I've gone to camp out so many times in my life—mainly in those seasons when still-here suffering and still-fresh grief and still-surprising pain interrupts my life. Those times when I know I have a stream of living water flowing from deep within me, but I don't feel like I do, because though Jesus has been glorified, He hasn't finished glorifying me yet. Though Jesus has removed the stains of my shame, I still think about them sometimes.

Revelation 21 is this too-good-to-be-true-but-the-truest-thing-there-is reminder that when this life is over, our shame won't just be undone but destroyed. Our sadness won't have the ability to resurface when we're weak because we won't be weak. We'll be fully new, fully quenched, fully whole.

> ***READ REVELATION 21:1-6.*** **Here we're reading John's vision of the new creation. What does John see in verse 1?**

Like many of you, as a child I thought—with great concern—that heaven would be everyone standing in rows, perhaps in coordinated robes, singing "I Could Sing of Your Love Forever," forever. I mean I liked the song, but I was hoping for a little more from my everlasting life. So I can't tell you the level of comfort that washed over me when I learned we wouldn't spend eternity as ghosty, bored spirits singing hymns. No. The Bible, right here, plain as day, tells us that there will be a new heaven and a new earth.

The things we love about earth, the created things we enjoy today, will be back but better than ever. NEW Chipotle bowls. BETTER Arnold Palmers.

All things will be new and improved because the sting of death and the consequences of sin will no longer be tainting them. Think about that!

What do these verses tell us about God's dwelling?

I'm about to go home for Christmas and am most excited to be with my family. I want to be full-body hugging my little sister in fuzzy socks by a fireplace. I want to hear my mom's laugh and watch my dad fight with their maltipoo over whatever she's got in her mouth. I want the with-ness. I want to be under their roof. What is better than dwelling with the people you love?

We get to have that with God but perfected. No conflict. No hurt feelings. No tiptoeing around differing worldviews or triggering topics. We will dwell with our Father, and He will dwell with us. Perfect family for all of forever.

***LOOK BACK AT VERSE 4*, and write it out in the space below, soaking in every word.**

I don't care how old you are, we all want someone bigger and stronger and better than us to wipe our tears and end our pain.

Go back up to what you just hand wrote and scribble out every word of what God tells us will pass away.

Death—gone; grief—goodbye; crying and pain because of things you've done or things you've had done to you, or things you've thought or things people have thought about you—passed away. Gone forever.

What a hope. What a joy. And it's true.

LOOK AT REVELATION 21:5 **and then flip back to 2 Corinthians 5:17. What do these verses both tell us?**

Those of us in Christ are new. We already are. We're not waiting till "then." We can already live free from shame when we remember and believe how powerful the forgiveness of God is. Whatever your shame is, whatever your sin is, it is forgiven, through the already-happened-death of Jesus, just as completely as it will be forgiven forever. The difference is that some day, not only will we be new but everything will be new. Everything. Our physical brains will be new. Our trauma-responses and memories and PTSD we carry with us—they will be gone.

For the Christian right now, your shame doesn't need to define you. In glory, your shame will have no opportunity to define you. Jesus will make EVERYTHING new.

What does the end of verse 6 tell us about the water of life (living water)?

What do these verses tell you about who God is, what He's like?

Our God is generous. Our God is holy. Our God has all the life and all the power and all the forgiveness and all the water. And He will give it freely to those of us who are His kids. In His home. Forever.

Close out this day at the well. Ask for the Holy Spirit, deep within you, to help you get through this pre-Revelation 21 day with a mind that is shame-free, joy-filled, and set on the love of Jesus.

WATCH

Write down any thoughts, verses, or things you want to remember as you watch the video for Session Three.

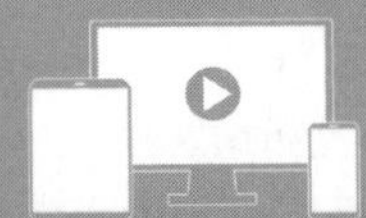

To access the video teaching sessions, use the instructions in the back of your Bible study book.

DISCUSS

The Samaritan woman may have carried shame because of her ethnicity and culture. Have you ever experienced anything like that?

This session's main idea is "Jesus gives living water to thirsty hearts." What did you learn in this session about living water and being quenched?

What are some things that you thirst for that will never satisfy?

In what ways do you identify with the woman at the well? How is your story similar to hers?

How can you help someone in your life see his or her need for living water this week?

PRAY

Thank God for making a way for us to be healed and whole and for giving us the most beautiful and hopeful Revelation 21 future. Pray specifically that God might provide opportunities for you to share the living water with others. Ask His Spirit to show you what that might look like individually and as a group.

FROM THIS WEEK'S STUDY

Review this week's memory verse.

Jesus said, "Everyone who drinks from this water will get thirsty again. But whoever drinks from the water that I will give him will never get thirsty again. In fact, the water I will give him will become a well of water springing up in him for eternal life."

JOHN 4:13-14

LEADING A GROUP?

A free leader guide PDF is available for download at **lifeway.com/ashamed**

SESSION FOUR

ASHAMED PETER

JESUS GIVES SECOND CHANCES

MEMORY VERSE

"FOLLOW ME," HE TOLD THEM, "AND I WILL MAKE YOU FISH FOR PEOPLE." **IMMEDIATELY THEY** LEFT THEIR NETS AND **FOLLOWED HIM.**

MATTHEW 4:19–20

(EMPHASIS ADDED)

DAY ONE

BEWARE THE SHAME REEL

Matthew 4:18–22; Luke 5:1–11; Matthew 14:22–33; Galatians 2:11–14

I don't know who came up with the term "shame reel," but it's something my husband and I refer to every once in a while. Like, "Oh, let's not talk about anything that happened in the 2006–2009 stretch of years. All of '06 to '09 is in the shame reel."

Note: Our wedding took place in 2006, and almost every part of that ceremony, other than the decision to be together, is considered, by us both, part of the shame reel.

We do our best to ignore, avoid, and erase all memories and evidence of those memories from our shared shame reel, including, but not limited to:

- Bad wedding hair (Both of us were guilty of this; his hair was Ringo Starr-ish, and mine was Lisa Marie Presley-like, even though it was 2006 and neither of us were alive in the '60s or '70s.)
- Being so uncomfortable and embarrassed during our "first dance" that we just stopped doing it after a few lines of the song
- The fact that no one told the pastor officiating our wedding where to stand, so he tried to hide in the fake plants that were on the altar, and in every single photo, you can see his head poking through the fake leaves

Also, there were the more intense struggles that day, many of them internal, including secret sins we were carrying and estranged family members who were not invited, among others.

You guys, we have never hung up a single picture from our wedding day. Why, you ask? Because why would we want to remember the cringiness of who we were and how we looked and what we were thinking back then?

Do you have anything like that in your reel? Hopefully, it's not your wedding day. But I think (I hope I'm not alone) everyone has core memories that make them grimace. Everyone has a "shame reel."

In the space below, share one of the most uncomfortable moments from your own personal shame reel. Feel free to use pig Latin, invisible ink, or just write it really tiny and then immediately scribble it out, so no one will see what you've written.

As the not-proud owner of a very robust shame reel (you are welcome to sample it in my most recent book, *You're the Worst Person in the World*, which is basically ten chapters of shame reels), I can't tell you how much comfort I find in the life of Peter.

Peter—fisherman, disciple Peter. Are you familiar with him? Refresher: He's the guy Jesus walked with and loved who was used by God to start the Christian church as we know it, AFTER so much shame-reel worthy behavior, and AFTER he literally denied even knowing Jesus, not once or twice but thrice. That guy. But I'm getting ahead of myself.

Let's start in Matthew.

OPEN YOUR BIBLE, AND READ MATTHEW 4:18-22. **What was Peter* doing when Jesus invited him to follow?**

*Note: Peter is also called Simon in the Bible. Simon is his actual name; Peter is a sort of nickname Jesus gave him later on. Sometimes you'll see him referred to as Simon or as Simon Peter or as Peter. Kind of like how sometimes my husband calls me Scarlet, but other times, at my request, he calls me "Savant Scrawls Prolific Author." That's how my name is saved in his phone, actually. I did it. I saved my name that way. Moving on.

How long did it take Peter to decide to follow Jesus?

Reflect on your own calling. If you're a follower of Jesus, how long did it take you to decide you were going to commit your life to Christ once you became aware of the truth of the gospel? What did that look like in your own life? If you're not a follower of Jesus, what drew you to pick up this Bible study? What is it about the story of Jesus calling people to Himself that attracts you?

READ LUKE 5:1-11. Many believe this is the same incident, described in two different Gospels.

How did Peter react in Luke's version of the story when Jesus miraculously filled his fishing nets with fish?

Do you remember how you responded when you first recognized God's power and holiness? What was your reaction?

In Session Two, we looked at a similar response to God's holiness in Isaiah 6. What do Isaiah's and Peter's responses have in common?

I love the similarity. I love how two totally different people—one a prophet, the other a fisherman—both fell before a perfect God and cried out about their sinfulness and unworthiness.

I've often been called out for being "self-deprecating." It's something I learned early on. It puts people at ease, for sure. Mostly, it puts me at ease!

It's also fun to make fun of yourself because you can be funny but at no one's expense but your own. You'll probably agree only having known me for a few sessions on paper and in video that it's my go-to.

But self-deprecation is not humility. Not even close. It's not godliness. It's a joke. It's a way to cope. It's actually kind of a mask.

True humility might sound similar, but it's beautifully different. Humility's motive isn't protection or relief or a laugh. Humility is free of motives altogether. It's just a sweet, surrendered recognition of our true condition and God's true greatness.

What similarities do you notice in how Jesus responds to Peter's humility with how God responded to Isaiah's?

In Isaiah, we see an explicit assurance of forgiveness. In Peter's story, we see an invitation to follow.

Bible scholar Thabiti Anyabwile makes such a powerful observation. He writes, "Uniquely, here is a holiness that comes to sinners. Rather than going away, Jesus says, 'Join me.' Here is a holiness that uses a confessing sinner in its mission. Here is holiness that not only calls the sinner but *commissions the sinner* to become a fisher of men. Here is holiness so stunningly beautiful it causes a man to leave everything for its sake. It gives the former sinner a new purpose, direction, and call."[1]

Jesus called Peter to fish for people (v. 10). Fishing for people is a metaphor for evangelism. So cool.

Jesus's metaphor was one Peter understood well as a fisherman. While the call to make disciples is for all of us who follow Jesus, Peter's call was delivered in a format specific to his current place in life.

How have you sensed God calling you to use your specific skills and place in life to fulfill your calling of disciple making? How have you seen others do that?

Are you pursuing the kingdom-focused things God has nudged you toward? If so, share in the space below. If not, what can you do this week to take a step in that direction?

As you read this next part, keep in mind that this is later in Peter's time as a disciple of Jesus. If you flip back beginning in Matthew 4, when Peter began following Jesus, you see all the rapid-fire miracles and huge events he was part of as he walked with Jesus. He saw miraculous healings (Matt. 4:23-25), the Sermon on the Mount (Matt. 5–7), Jesus calming a storm (Matt. 8:23-27), John the Baptist's beheading, and the feeding of the five thousand (Matt. 14:1-2). That's a lot.

***READ MATTHEW 14:22-33.* List out all the emotions you imagine the disciples, and specifically Peter, experienced while this was happening.**

What are a few reasons Peter might have experienced shame in this passage?

Oftentimes, shame isn't just a feeling you have internally when one of your many screen-distractions runs out of battery. Shame can be public.

And doesn't that make it exponentially more awful? When Peter's focus was on the power of Jesus, he got to experience a miracle. But, as soon as he took his eyes off Jesus and put them back on the storm, he started sinking. And all the disciples witnessed him sink.

READ GALATIANS 2:11-14 **(keeping in mind that "Cephas" is yet another name for Peter). In this passage, what is Paul calling Peter out for?**

Peter was being hypocritical in this passage. The CSB Study Bible calls it "fear-based hypocrisy."[2] Despite the fact that Peter had received a vision from God instructing him to fellowship with Gentiles, he allowed the opinions of others to sway his behavior, which in turn swayed the other believers around him.

Do you ever find yourself behaving differently or hiding things or (cough cough, hi!) being self-deprecating because you are overly concerned with what other people think of you?

There's so much we can learn from Peter's life as we seek to live lives free of shame, isn't there? When we look at the people around us or the storms we're in or the fish we need to catch, we'll sink, we'll be embarrassed, or we'll behave in ways we're ashamed of. But what happens when we look at our Savior? For Peter, it was literally looking at Jesus's face. For us today, it's not quite that literal.

How can we look to Jesus when we feel shame?

And what happens when we do? We experience peace, salvation, and miracles.

Close out this day by asking Jesus—the Remover of our shame, the Holy One who comes to sinners—to help you fix your eyes on Him today, not on your shame reel or future fears or tasks at hand.

DAY TWO

KITTEN POSTERS ON DETERMINATION

Matthew 16:13–18

I went to school in the nineties and early aughts when motivational posters were a real and prevalent part of everyday life. Nowadays, with all the nineties throwback, I see Gen Z poking their fun (I'm for you Gen Z and am a quiet appreciator of your TikTok humor), making insulting or ho-hum quotes into "motivational phone backgrounds." But, when the glossy paper posters lined the walls of my Christian high school, there was nothing ironic about them.

I remember a giant poster of a kitten hanging off the side of a cliff with the word "DETERMINATION," or something like that, in all caps. Most of the posters were forgettable or painfully cheesy, but there was one that I pondered when class felt boring. One that would cross my mind at night when I was trapped in my existential, angsty swirl.

It was hanging over the big white board in my history teacher's class, and all it said was what I now know is a quote attributed to Einstein: "What is right is not always popular; what is popular is not always right." And I remember that teacher explaining that if everyone is happy with you, you are probably not actually living for Jesus.

I stressed about whether or not it was okay that I was mildly popular (after having been severely unpopular). I wondered if Jesus could possibly be pleased with me/accept me/love me even though I wasn't actively being persecuted as one of His followers.

> **Think about the people in your life who don't follow Jesus. Who do you think they would say Jesus is?**

How would you answer the question, "Who do you say that I am?" if Jesus were to ask you right now?

NOW, READ MATTHEW 16:13-16. **When Jesus asked Peter what people said about who He was, how did Peter respond?**

My first few years of being a Christian, I wrestled so much with assurance of my salvation. I longed for a formula that would guarantee my saved status, but I lived life so consumed with my image of what people thought of me—the teacher with the motivational posters, my peers, my parents—that I often found my good works were self-centered. I wondered if I really, truly could claim Jesus as the Messiah or if I really, truly only wanted to do what it seemed "good girls" did.

READ MATTHEW 16:17. **Who does Jesus tell Peter was responsible for him recognizing that Jesus was the Messiah?**

Isn't that so comforting? Peter didn't believe because he was a super-awesome five-star person that all the fishermen admired. He believed, not because flesh and blood revealed it to him, but God in heaven.

In the space below, copy verse 17 down, and meditate on the beauty that God is the Revealer and the Savior and the Keeper of your soul.

READ MATTHEW 16:18-19. **Make a list of all the things Jesus said he would do through and for Peter.**

Look up the verses in the chart below, and make note of what Jesus promises He will do in and through and for His followers.

PASSAGE	WHAT JESUS WILL DO FOR YOU
Isaiah 40:31	
Matthew 16:24-25	
John 14:27	
John 15:9-15	
John 16:13-14	
Romans 5:10	
1 John 1:9	

Jesus offers us life, joy, peace, forgiveness, reconciliation—all the good stuff we long for.

We don't have to live in fear of what other people think or be ashamed of the times we've taken our eyes off of Jesus. Instead, we remember what He has revealed to us. He's given us eyes to see who He is. He's given us promises of what He will do. God reveals Himself to us, calls us, saves us, and does the work of transforming us into His likeness, bit by bit.

Close out this day thanking God for carrying the weight of your sins and the shame of your past, and praise Him for the beautiful future He has in store for all of us sinners who believe.

DAY THREE

PETER DENIES JESUS

Matthew 26:31–35,69–75; John 18:15–18; Romans 5:6–8

The only thing I've ever been good at predicting has been how long pets would thrive in our home. I have three little girls, and we've tested out most variety of animals. The most recent death I predicted was that of a caterpillar my youngest found on the patio. He had a name, a specified jar, and a collection of leaves. But he was a goner. I knew it immediately.

I gave him three days max. He made it two.

Caterpillar life spans might be my only area of expertise when it comes to conjecture. In today's passage though, we'll look at a prediction Jesus made about Peter and how that played out. Hint: Jesus is always right.

READ MATTHEW 26:31-35. **What prediction did Jesus make in these verses?**

What was Peter's reaction to Jesus's prediction?

If you were Peter in this moment, what emotions would you feel?

You know, I never think much about the fact that not only did Jesus love and use and save Peter after his three-time denial (as we'll discuss later), but He called it! He knew Peter would deny Him. The whole time Peter followed Jesus, He spoke salvation and promise and hope and purpose over Peter, BEFORE Peter failed Him. He did so KNOWING Peter would fail Him. Does that comfort your wound-up-tight-overthinking mind like it does mine?

What is something you carry shame about in this season of your life?

Hear me out here: Consider the reality that Jesus knew you'd fail the way you did before it even happened. And He called you to Himself anyway. He is calling you to Himself anyway, right now as you read this. In this way, we have an advantage over Peter. We know the end of the story. We know Jesus died and rose again to declare us forgiven and clean and His.

READ ROMANS 5:6-8. **When did Jesus die for us? (hint: while we were still ________________)**

How can we be ashamed when we remember that He loved before we loved? How can we ruminate on our failures when Jesus declared us forgiven and clean and His WHILE WE WERE STILL SINNERS?

READ MATTHEW 26:69-75. **When Peter was accused of being one of Jesus's followers, how did he respond?**

Has there ever been a time in your life you were dishonest in order to distance yourself from a person or situation that embarrassed you or made you feel threatened? Explain.

What do you think Jesus wants to say to your heart about that situation?

John's account of this same moment gives us a little more context.

***READ JOHN 18:15-18.* Note Peter's surroundings at this moment. Where was he? What details does John give about what Peter may have been smelling, feeling, hearing?**

It was Peter who cut off the soldier's ear when Jesus was being arrested (v. 10), and just a few verses later, he's denying Jesus completely.

Bring the burdens of your past failures to the Lord. Thank Him for His forgiveness, and copy Psalm 103:12 in the space below.

Looking at the denials of Peter reminds me of so many times my fear of man overpowered my belief in the all-powerful Jesus. In his book, *When People are Big and God is Small*, Edward T. Welch writes,

> *We fear people because they can*
>
> 1. *expose and humiliate us,*
> 2. *ridicule and reject us, and*
> 3. *attack, threaten, or oppress us.*
>
> *These three reasons have one thing in common: they see people as "bigger" (that is, more powerful and significant) than God, and, out of the fear that creates in us, we give other people the power to tell us what to feel, think, and do.*[3]

As you close out this day, write a prayer below, asking God to help you see how much bigger and more powerful He is than the people He created. Ask Him to help you live in light of that and ask for His help in fighting the shame you feel over actions you took when you made people big and God small.

DAY FOUR

SHAME-REVERSING POWER

John 21:1–19

The passage you are about to read is so beautiful. It has shame-reversing power. Open up to John 21. In this chapter, Jesus has already been crucified and buried. He's already risen from the dead, securing life for those who believe, and He has started visiting with people before ascending into heaven.

John 21 isn't just a random conversation Jesus had during His ministry. This conversation between Jesus and Peter that we're about to look at happened after Christ's ministry on earth, after He was mocked and tortured and killed for the salvation of humanity, and after Peter had denied Him, swearing and cursing (Matt. 26:74) that he didn't know the man.

So, get your mind there. Imagine, as you read, that you are Peter, and you're having an actual in-person conversation over breakfast with your back-from-the-dead Teacher/Friend/Savior, whom you denied, and denied, and denied again.

READ JOHN 21:1-14. **How is this similar to the story we read in Luke 5 of Peter's calling to follow Jesus?**

Describe some of what Peter might have been experiencing physically at this moment. What could he smell? What could he feel?

What moments from his past might those sensations bring to mind? Do you think those are pleasant memories for him?

When we carry shame in our hearts, we may avoid good things to avoid remembering the times when we failed, right? Peter, dripping wet from his swim in the sea, walked up to a charcoal fire Jesus had prepared for His disciples' breakfast.

Science tells us that smell, memory, and emotion are closely tied together due to the anatomy of our brains.[4] John specifically mentions a charcoal fire in John 18 and 21. These two instances are the only two times in the whole Bible where that phrase is used. Charcoal fires have a specific odor. Love it or hate it, you can probably remember a time you've been around a charcoal fire. Maybe a summer barbecue comes to mind for you.

The Bible does not explicitly say this, and I want to be clear on that, but I believe our Creator is intimately knowledgeable about how our brains work. He created brains, after all! He knows the memories we have associated with each smell. How beautiful and gracious that He would give Peter the opportunity to reset those memory connections in his mind!

***READ JOHN 21:15-19.* What was the question Jesus asked Peter?**

How many times did He ask it?

You know when you get into an argument with your spouse or a sibling or friend? Arguments, misunderstandings, or conflict, if serious enough, can fracture relationships beyond repair. You don't have to travel too far from the preschool playground to learn that. Conflict can destroy affection. So, what a blow it must have been for Peter to be asked by Jesus, "Do you love me?" Peter stood by the fire, hearing this question, knowing how he'd failed Jesus just before His death, and likely remembered that Jesus had predicted that's what he would do.

I can look back on my life and remember multiple situations where I wronged someone and then was faced with the reality that they'd witnessed it or heard about it. I'd been made.

I think of the time in sixth grade that some kids were making fun of one of my friends, and instead of defending him, I laughed. And then I realized he was standing right behind me.

I think of other times in my adult life that are too painful to write into a book where I said something about someone that wasn't honoring, and it got back to them.

In the top two instances that come to my mind, I didn't receive forgiveness from them. My actions ended our friendship. A just consequence for my failures. But here we see Peter and Jesus and they're together. They're eating breakfast. Peter knows that he is unworthy. Undeserved restoration.

REREAD VERSE 17. **When Jesus symbolically asked Peter "Do you love me" for the third time, how does the Bible say Peter felt?**

Every time I have been confronted with how my own mistakes have wronged someone else, I have felt that gut-wrenching sort of grief. It's like dropping a precious heirloom and watching it shatter into a million pieces, beyond repair.

How did Jesus respond three times to Peter's declaration?

Despite the grief and shame Peter undoubtedly carried, Jesus gave Him a role, a purpose, and a second chance.

In some translations, it's "Feed my sheep." In others, it's "lambs." The translation from the Greek is a little complex, but all of it points to shepherding, tending to, etc.

Now, in the same way He wasn't earlier telling Peter to cast a physical net in the ocean to "fish for people," Jesus wasn't talking about literal sheep needing breakfast.

So, what does sheep feeding look like in your life? Do you have children at home to disciple? A mentee at your church? If nothing comes to mind immediately, ask God to show you what it would look like for you to feed sheep.

Look at the last two words in verse 19. What did Jesus tell Peter to do?

If you flip back to Day One to that first passage we studied (Matt. 4:18-22), you can see how beautifully full circle this "Do you love me . . . feed my sheep" moment was for Peter.

What did Jesus say to Peter and his brother, Andrew, in Matthew 4:19, when they first met?

Isn't that amazing? Jesus said the same exact thing on both occasions. "Follow me." The same command. Peter was called by Jesus to follow Him and fish for people and feed sheep. Even when he messed it all up, he was not disqualified from serving Jesus. Even when his actions could have destroyed the relationship, Jesus kept Peter in His purpose and His love.

Can you think of an area of your life where your failures or mistakes have caused you to feel disqualified? Close out this day by writing out a prayer of renewed commitment to feed the sheep God has called you to feed and follow Him where He leads you. Thank Him for second and third and millionth chances, and move forward with gospel-given joy.

DAY FIVE

HOW GOSPEL-POWERED HUMILITY ERASES SHAME

1 Peter 5:6–11

> *Casting all your cares on him, because he cares about you.*
>
> 1 PETER 5:7

I used to be so frustrated by this verse. I wanted to experience it. I wanted to obey it. I just didn't understand it. Many times I tried casting, but I couldn't stop caring. I'd throw up my figurative arms, full of figurative cares and wonder why the peace thing wasn't kicking in.

But as I've learned to release my shame, I've also learned to embrace God's Word. I've learned that studying Scripture slowly and routinely and fully is not a box to check, but it's the very key to transformation—the very way to make peace with my past.

It wasn't until I looked one verse before verse 7 that I understood how to cast my cares on the Lord and why I even could.

READ 1 PETER 5:6-7. **Copy the first two words you see in the space below. (If the version you're using puts a "Therefore" or a "So" at the beginning, skip that word and write the next two).**

Shame and humility are antonyms that we often treat like synonyms. As we discussed on Day One of this session, being humble isn't wallowing in humiliation; it's having an awareness of your true status in light of God's goodness. Isn't it so beautiful, then, that Peter is the one who wrote these verses, under the inspiration of the Holy Spirit? Peter, aware of Jesus's divinity, aware of how he'd failed his friend, and aware that he'd been forgiven and given a second chance said, "Humble yourselves, therefore, under the mighty hand of God, so that he may exalt you at the proper time."

We can all personalize that.

In the space below, humble yourself. Write down a few memories of times you've seen the mighty hand of God at work in your life.

If you look again at verse 7 in light of verse 6, it is so much easier to cast your cares. Casting is really about remembering who is in control. We can humble ourselves, surrendering the cares we can't carry ourselves, when we remember and believe the gospel. I love how Tim Keller explains the life-changing power of the gospel. It came across my Facebook® feed again just this morning.

> *The Christian Gospel is that I am so flawed that Jesus had to die for me, yet I am so loved and valued that Jesus was glad to die for me. This leads to deep humility and deep confidence at the same time. It undermines both swaggering and sniveling.*[5]

If you picked this Bible study up, you might feel that you're more prone to the "sniveling." You might feel far from swagger and overwhelmed with shame. Or maybe you got pressured into coming to this study, and you actually feel like you're doing pretty awesome. The incredible thing is that the "deep humility" Keller references here gets us away from both of those two unhealthy extremes and gives us a confidence that comes from the gratitude of being given the world-changing grace of Jesus.

READ 1 PETER 5:8-11. **In concluding his letter, what warning does Peter give in verses 8 and 9?**

Having studied Peter's relationship with Jesus, why is this significant?

You probably wouldn't take parenting advice from someone who's never had kids. Or how about violin lessons from someone who has never played? It's a lot easier for us to take someone's advice when they've got experience. Honestly, I studied 1 Peter all my life in Christian schools and college, but I never considered who was writing the letter. I never considered that the one urging me to resist the devil and stand firm in my faith was someone who hadn't resisted, someone who hadn't always stood firm. Peter wasn't a mom-blogger with no children of his own. When he writes about prowling lions and suffering and resisting, he knows what he's talking about.

What hope does Peter offer in verses 10-11?

How stunning. How powerful. The guy who denied Jesus, who cowered in fear rather than standing firm gives us a warning, followed by incredible comfort. God will "restore, establish, strengthen, and support [us] after [we] have suffered a little while."

Using what you learned this week, how did we see Peter experience restoration, establishment, strengthening, and support?

Have you experienced these comforts after struggling with shame? In the space below, try to recall and record times you have experienced these gifts from the Lord.

Restoration:

Establishment:

Strengthening:

Support:

Close out this day, thanking God for these good gifts we have because of the mercy of Jesus.

VIEWER GUIDE | SESSION FOUR

WATCH

Write down any thoughts, verses, or things you want to remember as you watch the video for Session Four.

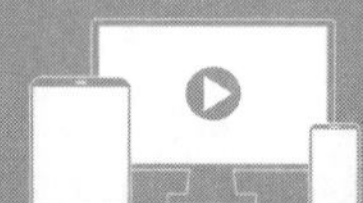

To access the video teaching sessions, use the instructions in the back of your Bible study book.

DISCUSS

On Day One, we read about when Jesus met Peter and said, "Follow me." Take some time to share about what your life looked like when you were introduced to Jesus.

This session's main idea is "Jesus gives second chances." If you're comfortable, share a testimony of a time God gave you a second chance.

Flip back to the chart you filled out on Day Two (p. 74), showing what Jesus promises to do in and through His followers. Which of these promises resonates most with you? Why?

In what ways do you personally identify with Peter? What, in your own history with the Lord, brings a feeling of shame to your mind? What have you learned that Jesus wants to do with your shame by studying Peter this week?

Jesus used Peter to build the church as we know it. If you're involved in your local church, how has God wired you to serve the body? If you're not yet involved, what do you sense God is leading you to do within your church?

FROM THIS WEEK'S STUDY

Review this week's memory verse.

"Follow me," he told them, "and I will make you fish for people." Immediately they left their nets and followed him.

MATTHEW 4:19-20

PRAY

Thank God for allowing His children to do kingdom work and live with purpose, even though we don't deserve that joy and privilege. Pray specifically that you, as a group, would walk in joyful obedience as you continue to study God's Word together. Ask that the Lord unite your group and remove all shame that is keeping you from service to Him and joy in His calling on your life.

LEADING A GROUP?

A free leader guide PDF is available for download at **lifeway.com/ashamed**

SESSION FIVE

ASHAMED PAUL

JESUS TAKES THE WORST OF US AND MAKES US WORTHY

MEMORY VERSE

THIS SAYING IS TRUSTWORTHY AND DESERVING OF FULL ACCEPTANCE. **"CHRIST JESUS CAME INTO THE WORLD TO SAVE SINNERS"** — AND I AM THE WORST OF THEM. BUT I RECEIVED **MERCY** FOR THIS REASON, SO THAT IN ME, THE WORST OF THEM, CHRIST JESUS MIGHT DEMONSTRATE HIS **EXTRAORDINARY PATIENCE** AS AN EXAMPLE TO THOSE WHO WOULD BELIEVE IN HIM FOR ETERNAL LIFE.

1 TIMOTHY 1:15–16

(EMPHASIS ADDED)

DAY ONE

SHIPWRECK TATTOOS ON SHIPWRECKED PEOPLE

Acts 9:1–19

I'm on a plane right now, leaving Atlanta. I was here to speak at a church event north of town and can't stop thinking about a testimony I heard.

One of my favorite things about traveling to speak and share my testimony is getting to talk to women before and after, getting to hear their stories of how Jesus has changed their lives.

Before I went up to speak at this church last night, a woman from the congregation got up to share her story. She had cool, chunky glasses, a spunky haircut, and a full sleeve of tattoos. "These tattoos are my testimony," she said.

The tattoos depicted a shipwreck. A shipwreck that represented the circumstances and outcome of a life that had let her down. But Jesus redeemed her. He healed her wounds and restored what was broken. She said that when she worships at church and raises her arms up, she can see the shipwreck tattoo turned upside down, and it reminds her how Jesus changed everything.

Her story was different from mine. The pain she'd experienced. The losses she'd grieved. But I couldn't help but feel like she was telling my story too. Jesus meets us in our brokenness—however our own personal brokenness takes shape.

This week we are looking at one of Scripture's biggest shipwreck-people-turned-apostle—Paul, also known as Saul. You've experienced shame in your past? For sure. You've done things or said things you hate remembering? You've *not* done things or *not* said things you keep recalling and regretting? The apostle Paul says to you, "Hold my grape juice." Paul was the worst, and Paul was made new. We can be encouraged by a persecutor turned martyr who just so happened to have gotten into some actual shipwrecks too.

READ ACTS 9:1-18. **What does verse 1 say that Paul (remember, Paul is Saul) was doing when he was traveling on this Damascus road?**

Pretty intense guy, this Saul/Paul was. Have you ever had so much anger in your heart that you were "breathing threats and murder" against people? Don't answer that.

When I first learned about Paul, I viewed him as a villain with a big life-changing story. But I didn't think about how Paul must have viewed himself, in his own eyes. From his perspective, his murderous threat-breathing was righteous! See, Paul was a Jew. He was part of the elite "God's chosen people" group, the Israelites. He was religious. In fact, he was so religious that he viewed himself as this holy warrior guy who would take down anyone who didn't worship his God his way.

When he heard about this group of people who followed Jesus—people who Paul and others like him thought were crazy, blasphemous, extremists—he justified violence as a way to remedy what he was seeing.

But his encounter with Jesus changed everything.

When Paul asked who the voice was, what answer did he receive?

I appreciate the clarity here, as I'm reading this centuries later as someone who has not hunted down Jesus followers to put them into prison. However, imagine how that answer felt to Paul. Not only is it (rightly) accusatory, but also Jesus equates Himself with His followers. He was essentially telling Paul: *You aren't just hurting people who believe in Me. You are persecuting Me. Jesus.*

LOOK AGAIN AT VERSES 10-18. **What was the name of the guy who God commanded to go help Paul?**

How did he respond when the Lord said his name in verse 10, and who does that remind you of from Session Two?

"Here I am, Lord!" "Here I am; send me!" Remember, Isaiah? Isn't it cool and beautiful that when regular people encounter God, their response is service rather than shame?

Ananias was willing to go serve a known murderer, a known persecutor, because God called him by name and told him to.

In verses 15-16, what did God tell Ananias about what would happen to Paul?

Why do you think God told Ananias these things about Paul's future?

LOOK AT ACTS 9:18. **What happened immediately before Paul got baptized?**

God opened Paul's eyes to His holiness, just like He did to Ananias, just like Isaiah, just like me. And Paul walked forward in joyful obedience, rather than wallowing in the failures of his past. Incredible.

What do you tend to do or turn to when you are confronted with your sin?

If you have an unhealthy pattern of getting stuck in the sadness of your failures, how might you learn from Paul's example?

Close out this day asking the Holy Spirit to show you how to behave differently in light of the reality that your sins are forgiven.

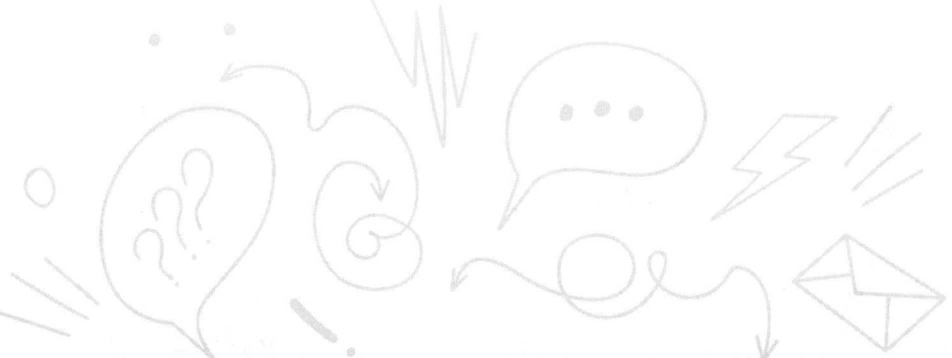

DAY TWO

THE ONLY FIX FOR BROKEN PEOPLE

Acts 9:20–31; Luke 18:27

I've dealt with a painful estrangement in my family on and off since I was eighteen years old. The hot and cold of it, the misunderstandings, the severing words and the crying and the praying and counseling and book dog-earring.

It has been one of the most heartbreaking and deflating things I've ever experienced. I hung around and tried again and again to fix something that wasn't getting fixed. I cycled through hurt and anger and frustration and exasperation and SHAME. So much shame. Aren't I a child of God? Shouldn't my supernatural love be able to fix what's broken? What's wrong with me? What's wrong with my faith?

The cynic in me (that can still pop up when I'm not careful) used to nod in world-weary agreement at the expression, "People never change." *Addicts will always be addicts. Cheaters will always cheat. Never trust a liar.*

And honestly, history and a little life experience often proves those things to be true. But God.

READ ACTS 9:20-25. **What did Paul immediately start doing after his conversion?**

Why were his listeners astounded?

I can't think of much else that is more powerful proof of a heart-changing God than encountering a heart-changed person. Sure, this side of heaven we'll always be weighed down by sin: redeemed addicts may still struggle against the source of their addiction, repentant cheaters may still feel a draw to cheat, and rescued liars could still feel tempted to lie. But the power of the gospel tells us that we're no longer enslaved to those sins because Jesus transforms us out of our slavery to sin. As Paul reminds us in 2 Corinthians 3:17, "Where the Spirit of the Lord is, there is freedom."

If you are a believer, do you remember how you used to live and function before you became a child of God? What were you like? What has changed?

READ ACTS 9:26-30. **How did Jesus's disciples respond to Paul when he tried to join them?**

Have you ever been wary of trusting someone who claimed to be changed? Why or why not?

All of us carry the pains of loving people who are making choices that hurt them and their relationships. A lot of those situations look hopeless and some of them even end in what appears to be hopelessness. Someone I love passed away last year. Addiction and depression led to suicide. The ultimate expression of hopelessness. I'll be honest—the pain of that aftermath makes it hard for me to believe that people can change. But though I carry stories of pain and loss, I've also witnessed the miracle of people headed down that path who were redeemed and restored like Paul.

What evidence did Barnabas give to explain Paul's transformation?

Have you ever seen a dramatic change, similar to Paul's, in someone's life? Maybe it was your own. What evidence would you give that that person had changed? What evidence would someone else give about your life?

Not only did Barnabas cite Paul's preaching "in the name of Jesus," he also said Paul "had seen the Lord." Paul literally saw Jesus. He saw his own sin in the light of the One who died to save him from those sins. And he left that encounter a changed man.

NOW, READ VERSE 31. **What happened to the churches in the area as Paul and the others who were changed by Jesus shared the good news?**

Not only did the church grow in numbers, but in strength and in peace. I love verse 31 so much. Praying for the lost, hoping for restoration and healing and unity—it's not in vain.

READ LUKE 18:27, **and copy it down below. Pay attention to each word and ask the Holy Spirit to help your heart believe it.**

The health of the church and the healing of broken people and relationships is not up to us and our frail hands. It is Jesus Christ who changes lives. He uses formerly hopeless people like me and Saul the Persecutor to do it. So, be encouraged. Forsake your shame. Hope in the transformative power of the gospel. Jesus is using you, and the kingdom of heaven can't be defeated.

Close out this day praying for those people you love in those relationships that hurt. Ask in faith for the Lord to strengthen and encourage you, your church, and community. Ask Him to help you have peace in the things you can't change and trust His power over the rest.

DAY THREE

COMPETENT WORSTIES

2 Corinthians 3:4–18; 4:1–6; 5:17

Last year, like I mentioned, I published a book called, *You're the Worst Person in the World.* I wrote ten chapters on my worstness, in hopes readers might see their own (and maybe laugh with me?). I really wanted #worsties to take off as a hashtag on Instagram, but alas, it has not. Apparently, nobody wants to celebrate being the worst.

But one of the things I love about Paul's ministry is the confidence his humility produced. He wasn't trying to hashtag his failures or toot a horn about his wins. His confidence didn't come from himself. That is so powerful because he was very qualified to be an extra-zealous Jew according to the standards of the time (Phil. 3:4-6).

The subheading in today's reading in my Bible is "Paul's Competence." When I see the word *competence*, I feel like I'm about to read a list of special braggy skills on someone's LinkedIn® profile.

To Whom It May Concern,

My name is Paul, and the following is but a sample of my skills and competencies . . .

- Inexhaustible Work-Ethic
- Collaborative Synergistic Leadership
- Prolific Written Communication Prowess
- Multi-lingual (Hebrew, Aramaic, Greek)
- Organizational Know-How
- Creative, Empathetic Multitasking
- Rabid Punctuality
- Working Knowledge of Microsoft Excel®

But Paul's second letter to the Corinthian church reads nothing like that.

READ 2 CORINTHIANS 3:4-6. **How does Paul say we are made competent? Why do we need to be made competent?**

In his letter to the Ephesians, Paul explains that salvation in Jesus is a gift, so no one can boast. But, here in 2 Corinthians, he reminds the church members of Corinth then, and us now, that we can't claim anything as having come from ourselves.

NOW, READ VERSES 7-11. **Why does Paul say the glory of the law given to Moses is less glorious than the ministry of the Spirit?**

If you didn't include it in your answer above, the most breathtaking difference between the law on stone tablets and the ministry of the Spirit is that the law condemned us all.

No one is able to keep the law perfectly. No one but the glorious, holy God Himself.

Paul goes so far as to tell us we have a front-row seat to God's glory on display through the work of Jesus and the presence of the Holy Spirit with us (2 Cor. 3:12-18).

Doesn't that front-row seat to God's glory on display give us boldness? Doesn't it remind us that Christ has removed the veil so that we can see God's glory more fully, as if a veil has been removed (2 Cor. 3:16)? It really does.

Seeing the fullness of God's glory reminds us of our need. It reminds us that we can never be worthy on our own. The glory of God, the glory of His covenant, will not fade. Because of this, we can stand boldly because we are "being transformed into the same image from glory to glory" through Jesus.

Speaking of testimony tattoos, I've got a Bible verse reference tattooed on my right wrist:

> *Therefore, if anyone is in Christ, he is a new creation; the old has passed away, and see, the new has come!*
>
> 2 CORINTHIANS 5:17

If you lose sight of that, you may find yourself living under condemnation from a law that you have already been forgiven for breaking. Whether or not you actually feel free of shame, if you have given your life to God and invited Jesus the Savior into your life, you are ALREADY free! You are ALREADY new! God's will for you isn't shame, it's glory. He doesn't want to make you hide; He wants to make you like Him.

READ 2 CORINTHIANS 4:1-6. **Why is it that we do not give up?**

What is it that we are to renounce?

What would it look like in your personal life if the gospel was unveiled?

See, fighting shame doesn't mean being "shameless" in the negative sense of the word. We who are in Christ know very well how undeserving we are. We know we couldn't live up to God's standard. We know our hearts are deceitful (Jer. 17:9). But we do not have to be ashamed. Jesus has made us clean! He's not overlooking your worstness. He's removed it, canceled it, and exchanged it for His best. We get to wear the blamelessness of Jesus. What a mercy.

Close out this day by writing a prayer of gratitude. Ask the Lord to help your heart's baseline have the joyful, peaceful rest of one who has truly been redeemed.

DAY FOUR

FIGHTING SHAME BY LOOKING UP

2 Corinthians 4:7–18; Colossians 3:2

Grandma Marlene, a rock in my family, died from COVID pneumonia last year. I got a phone call that she was in the hospital, and while I was talking with my husband, trying to decide if I should make plans to fly across the country and go see her, I got a second call that she wasn't going to make it and a nurse from the hospital could FaceTime® me and hold the phone up so I could say goodbye. I pulled my car over in the parking lot of an apartment complex I happened to be driving by and sobbed as I saw her face on my phone screen, mostly obscured by an oxygen mask.

I frantically took screen shots, struggling to believe that I'd never see her face again. I still have them on my phone. Probably one hundred images that all look the same.

Someone, my mom or the nurse, had Grandma's hair done in two braids on the side of her head. I didn't know what to say. All I remember coming out was "I love you so much, Grandma. Your braids are so pretty. I love you. I love you. I love you. Thank you, Jesus, for my Grandma. Thank you, Jesus . . ."

She died a few minutes later.

My heart is still broken over her death because I miss her presence here. But the way she lived gives me so much confidence in the eternity she always talked about and longed for.

Something she lived by and taught me was Colossians 3:2. "Set your minds on things above, not on earthly things." That was her secret. That was where her near-constant joy came from.

Her life circumstances were up and down, but she lived a life full of gratitude. She raved about trees in her yard and birds in her bird bath. She sang songs to Jesus and walked around with a unique and radiant confidence because her mind was set on eternal things.

We used to joke with her about how much she loved her "treasures." She was a doll collector and visiting her house was like going to a museum. But Jesus was clearly, undeniably the treasure of her soul.

When I read today's passage, written by Paul, under the inspiration of the Holy Spirit, I think about the life I watched Grandma Marlene live out to the very end. I want you to have the same radiant confidence and joy that Jesus gave her.

READ 2 CORINTHIANS 4:7-18. **In the chart below, use today's passage to record our state in light of each circumstance. I'll do the first one for you.**

THOUGH WE ARE . . .	WE ARE . . .
Afflicted in every way	Not crushed
Perplexed	
Persecuted	
Struck down	

Which of these realities feels most applicable in your life right now? Whichever one it is, copy down what you wrote in the box and how it applies to your situation. (For example, someone might write: "I am afflicted in every way. I'm not getting along with my brother, my car just died, I missed out on a promotion; but I am not crushed because God is . . . ")

NOW, ZERO IN ON VERSE 10. **What does that verse say we carry in our bodies and what then can be displayed in our bodies?**

Last year, when I lost Grandma Marlene, I suffered so many other afflictions. We buried my Uncle Jimmy (her son) who died by suicide just sixteen days earlier. We had just moved across the country, away from our friends, family, support system, all of it. We had health struggles and mental health struggles and all kinds of struggles that year. Afflicted in every way . . .

But not crushed.

We all carry the curse with us, don't we? We live in a world broken by sin, a world tainted with shame. If you didn't feel it pre-2020, you feel it now. A phrase I used to describe myself during that season of loss and affliction was "world weary." We are world weary, but we are never without hope.

LOOK AT VERSES 14 AND 15. **What does Paul say can extend through us?**

Where does the thanksgiving at the end of verse 15 come from?

Jesus's resurrection changed everything. The ultimate curse of our sin is death, and when He came back to life, He showed the world His power over it. If God can raise Jesus from the dead, if God can forgive the sins of Paul the persecutor, can't He forgive you? Can't He heal you from how others have sinned against you? Of course He can. He has world-making power. Jesus-resurrecting power. And He uses that power to love us. Setting our minds on this amazing reality produces what verse fifteen says it will—it produces gratitude. It makes us thankful people. And we can't be thankful and shameful at the same time.

I love looking at Colossians 3:2 and 2 Corinthians 4:18 side by side. We can set our minds on things above, focus on eternity, on the goodness of the Lord, on the unseen because while the things that have brought us shame are temporary, the love of our all-powerful God through Jesus is forever.

Finish today's time with Jesus by reflecting back on 2 Corinthians 4:16-18. Pray a prayer, reminding yourself exactly why it is that we do not give up—exactly why it is that we can shake off shame, hold on to thankfulness, and hope in the power of God.

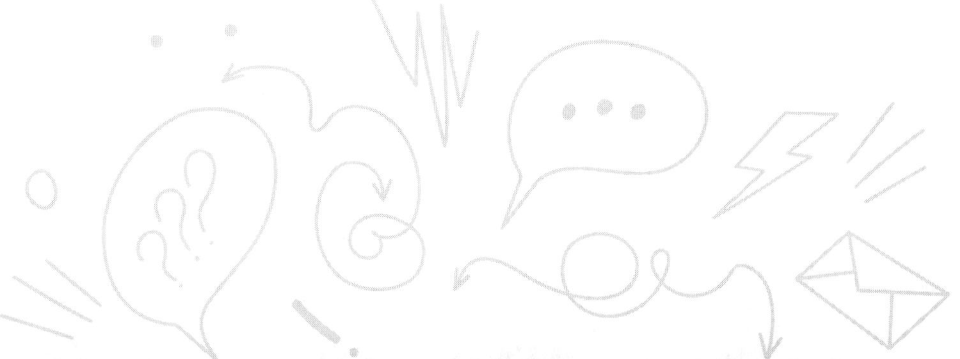

DAY FIVE

SHAME TURNED TESTIMONY

1 Timothy 1:12–17

Today's passage has a beautiful heading in my CSB Bible: "Paul's Testimony." Man, I love hearing people's testimonies. I love the colorful ones like Paul's and the ones that point to faithful families passing down the good news.

The older I get, the more testimonies of my own I rack up.

I was a fourteen-year-old striver who saw her neediness and made a commitment to Jesus.

Then I was an anorexic bulimic who was healed and shown mercy by a powerful God.

Then, I was a panicked new mom who wanted comfort and protection more than I wanted God, and He reminded me of His love for me and my purpose in Him.

Then, I was a world-weary woman, too tired and too sad and too grieving to pursue the Lord, but He used people and prayer and His Word to pursue me and hold me and give me joyful endurance.

God is constantly turning brokenness into beauty. He turns shame into testimonies.

> ***READ 1 TIMOTHY 1:12-17.* What words did Paul use to describe who he was before?**

Can you identify with any of those descriptions? If so, write about it below. What did your specific struggles look like before you were changed by Jesus? If you don't know Him yet, what is weighing you down right now?

How did Paul describe what changed him?

Why did Paul say he received mercy?

How might your own testimony demonstrate God's "extraordinary patience"?

"'Christ Jesus came into the world to save sinners'—and I am the worst of them." What a stunningly beautiful sentiment when it's spoken in earnest. But what a difficult thing to admit.

We spend our entire lives justifying bad behavior and trying to convince ourselves that we're worthy. Or we distract ourselves away from thinking about it, but the reality is, it's not working. And it takes a lot of mental gymnastics to try to convince ourselves that we're good people.

After Paul's encounter with Jesus, he had the truth figured out. He was physically blinded, but his eyes were opened to his need, his weakness, his glaring failure of letting self-righteousness consume him.

He was finally able to see the giant Jesus-sized need in his life, and Jesus was there to fill it.

What a wonder that when we are able to be honest with ourselves about our own weaknesses, we are most poised to be free.

> *Do you have a testimony? A God story? A "I was this, but now I'm that" to share? Try to put it into words in the space provided. If you're a visual person, draw a picture here or on the next page of what your life looked like before Christ and how following Him changed it.*

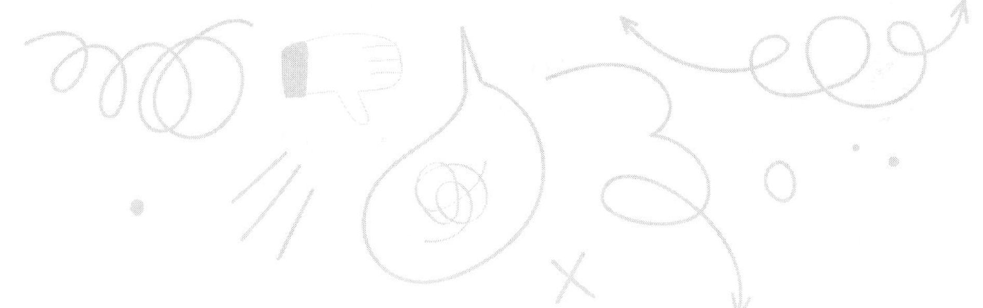

WATCH

Write down any thoughts, verses, or things you want to remember as you watch the video for Session Five.

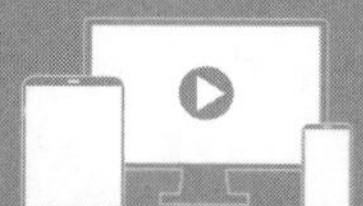

To access the video teaching sessions, use the instructions in the back of your Bible study book.

DISCUSS

This week, we studied Paul and his one hundred eighty degree turn of a testimony. What is the most dramatic one eighty type of testimony you've ever heard?

This session's main idea is "Jesus takes the worst of us and makes us worthy." When have you gotten to a point where you had to acknowledge your "worstness?"

Do you have a Grandma Marlene in your life? Someone who, though imperfect, showed you what it looks like to live in light of eternity? Describe that person.

PRAY

Thank God for forgiving sinners like us and allowing us to take part in the beautiful love story He's writing. Thank Him for saving people like Paul. Thank Him for the one hundred eighty degree testimonies and the quieter ones. Thank Him for what He is doing in your story and in your group. Spend the remainder of your time in prayer. Pray specifically, that you, as a group, would spend the rest of this week reflecting the unveiled gospel, with hearts free of shame.

FROM THIS WEEK'S STUDY

Review this week's memory verse.

This saying is trustworthy and deserving of full acceptance: "Christ Jesus came into the world to save sinners" — and I am the worst of them. But I received mercy for this reason, so that in me, the worst of them, Christ Jesus might demonstrate his extraordinary patience as an example to those who would believe in him for eternal life.

1 TIMOTHY 1:15-16

LEADING A GROUP?

A free leader guide PDF is available for download at **lifeway.com/ashamed**

SESSION SIX

SHAME CRUCIFIED

JESUS EXPERIENCED OUR SHAME SO WE DON'T HAVE TO

MEMORY VERSE

THEREFORE, SINCE WE ALSO HAVE SUCH A LARGE CLOUD OF WITNESSES SURROUNDING US, **LET US LAY ASIDE EVERY HINDRANCE AND THE SIN THAT SO EASILY ENSNARES US.** LET US **RUN WITH ENDURANCE** THE RACE THAT LIES BEFORE US, **KEEPING OUR EYES ON JESUS**, THE PIONEER AND PERFECTER OF OUR FAITH. FOR THE JOY THAT LAY BEFORE HIM, HE ENDURED THE CROSS, DESPISING THE SHAME, AND SAT DOWN AT THE RIGHT HAND OF THE THRONE OF GOD.

HEBREWS 12:1–2

(EMPHASIS ADDED)

DAY ONE

WE ARE GUILTY

Romans 1:16–32; 3:9–24

After Jesus changed the apostle Paul's life, Paul spent the rest of it traveling around, as the Holy Spirit led, sharing the gospel and building the church. Remember, this is the same guy whose past involved imprisoning Jesus's followers and even having them killed. But God took his zeal and redirected it. He took Paul's sin and forgave it.

Paul had so many failures and sins he could have looked back on, but instead he preached the good news of Jesus with confidence. Paul knew his past, so he wasn't confident in himself. He was confident in his Savior.

READ ROMANS 1:16-17. **What is Paul "not ashamed" of?**

Have you ever found yourself ashamed of the gospel, or embarrassed to share your faith? Why do you think that is?

NOW, READ ROMANS 1:18-25. **What do these verses say about our guilt?**

Perhaps that's not the most encouraging passage. But it is crucial and true.

When we're faced with the gospel, we see that we are guilty. We deserve God's wrath. It's true. We are "without excuse," because just like this description in Romans, we have so many times lacked gratitude, walked in darkness, worshiped things that are not God. And that means, in so many ways, that the shame we feel isn't groundless. Which only makes it more amazing when God makes it go away.

READ ROMANS 1:26-32. **What stands out to you? Write down any of the unrighteous things in that list that you currently struggle with.**

It's a painful list to read. I can say confidently that some of that resonates with me. We are wired to worship, and if we aren't worshiping the One who is worthy, we will worship ourselves. That leads to the pursuit of the things in that long list, which inevitably leads to guilt and shame.

NOW READ ROMANS 3:9-20. **According to this passage, is anyone justified by the works of the law?**

Have you ever lived like you could be justified by your works? What did that look like in your life?

READ ROMANS 3:21-24. **Be honest; have you ever read verse 24 before?**

I ask that because Romans 3:23 is a key verse in the Christian faith. I could have probably told you "all have sinned and fall short of the glory of God" before I understood what any of those eleven words mean. As is so often the case in Christianity, if you don't study the Scriptures, you may find yourself memorizing halves of sentences and leaving off the most important and life changing parts.

REREAD ROMANS 3:23-24. **What good news do we find in verse 24?**

We are justified! We are made absolutely sinless before God. Not by adhering to the law. Not by being super pretty or super smart or super nice or having a super empty shame reel. We are justified by the grace of God through the redemption that is in Christ Jesus.

Today, pray that the Lord will keep you from living for the law, from worshiping your own self and your own will. Ask Him to flood you with the knowledge and joy that you are justified. You do not have to live ashamed of your past sins or ashamed of the gospel.

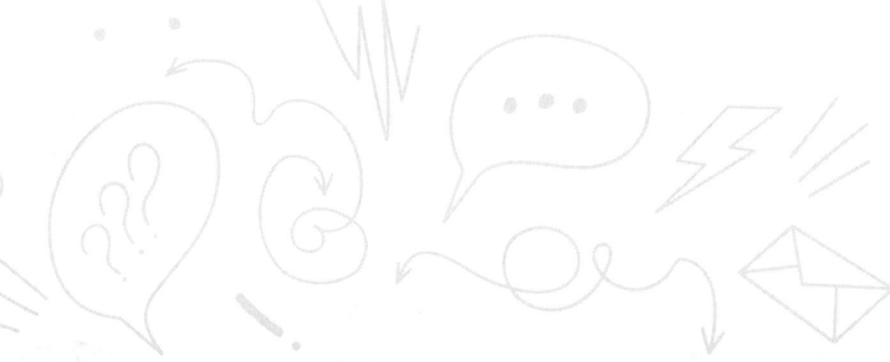

DAY TWO

SPECIAL GUESTS AT ODYSSEY

Romans 5:1–11; 6:1–2

My oldest daughter, Ever, is a faithful and frequent listener of an almost forty-year-old radio program from Focus on the Family called *Adventures in* Odyssey®.

I remember hearing the show when I was little. Sometimes, at my Christian school, we'd watch an *Adventures in Odyssey* cartoon. But, today, it's a whole, huge THING.

There's something called "AIO Club," and it's an app that streams all of the over eight hundred episodes of the show. complete with devotionals, fan art pages, and badges you can earn for listening to a lot of episodes. They even send a monthly magazine.

My Ever, when she does things, she does them all the way. She is an AVID AIO member. She listens to the episodes while crafting in all her spare time, has had her fan art featured on the app, etc. She's obsessed. And I think, as far as obsessions go, it's a pretty healthy one.

I learned that not only was Odyssey a radio show, but they've designed a place kids can visit, complete with a three-story-slide, recording studio they can record a little take-home episode in, a restaurant that mirrors the one in the show, with the Wod-Fam-Choc-Sod (world famous chocolate soda) on the menu and everything.

So, you can imagine my desperation to bring my daughters when I found out I was going to be a guest on *Focus on the Family* to talk about one of my books.

Needless to say, I brought my kids. They got to do the Odyssey experience and had a special tour of the real studio. My eleven-year-old got to pitch an episode idea to one of the writers. (If you ever hear about a new character on the show that is a lionhead rabbit named Puffy, you'll know where that idea came from.)

That day in Colorado Springs, my daughter had unique and special access to one of her favorite things.

She was so ecstatic even though she did nothing to earn it. She didn't win a "greatest fan" competition. Someday she might have the most AIO badges but not yet. She partied in Odyssey, not because of her awesomeness, but because she's my daughter, and I happened to be going to Odyssey for work.

That's what happens to us, but on the scale of infinity, when we become the children of the Creator of literally everything. We have access to the Kingdom of God, not because we are incredible but because we are His kids.

READ ROMANS 5:1-5. **Why do we have peace with God?**

In verse 2, what (rather, whom) does our faith give us access to?

Because of all this, we can "boast" in our afflictions. Why?

Being a child of God means we get access to Him, His Kingdom, His friendship. It's better than chocolate sodas and new episodes on Thursdays and meeting the writers behind the scenes. Access to God means peace and hope and fulfillment. Access to God means freedom from fear and pain and sin and shame! Daughter of God, that is for you. HE is for you. Like Paul writes in verse 5, our hope will not disappoint us because God is more than just a cool thing or a cool person; He IS love, and He pours that love into our hearts through His Spirit. Wow.

CONTINUE READING VERSES 6-11. **When did Christ die for the ungodly?**

What does it mean for us that Christ died for us while we were still sinners?

God didn't wait until we earned our own worthiness. He didn't wait until next week when we get our acts together. He didn't look around and say, "Okay, now everyone is good enough for me to send Jesus." Christ died for us while we were still sinners. While we still bore our shame and guilt and ungodliness and unworthiness.

What does verse 11 say we boast in?

Boasting in our afflictions and boasting in God may sound very different at first. How do we boast in both?

When we boast in our afflictions, we do so because we know that God uses them to refine us. And, like we learned last week, we know that because of Jesus, we will not be crushed by them. Instead, they will produce hope in us. Boasting in that hope is boasting in God—the One who makes all things new, who is our hope.

***READ ROMANS 6:1-2.* What question does Paul ask and answer in these verses?**

What a gift that our sin is forgiven and our shame is conquered. But Paul reminds us here not to live like it doesn't matter what we do once we're in Christ. We are set free from shame, and so we are then able to strive for God's glory—not in an effort to earn anything but because we love Him and our obedience and desire for righteousness reflects that.

So, are you starting to see it? Are you starting to see whatever it is that brings you shame shrink down in light of this gift? Whatever it is, it can't compare to the authority of God. And God says it is gone. So we don't boast in our ability to avoid the bad stuff that makes us feel ashamed. We boast in God who has made us no longer shameful. Instead, He's made us His.

Today, pray to God like you're talking to a friend. If you've made the decision to follow Jesus, God is your friend! You don't have to avoid Him when you fail. You can bring whatever you are and whatever you've done to Him, knowing with confidence that He can handle it; He has handled it. Talk to Him, knowing with confidence that He will not shut you out or turn you away or humiliate you.

DAY THREE

THE SOLUTION

Romans 8:1–11

Many years ago, the Southern Baptist association of Miami, Florida gave land to start a hospital called Baptist Hospital. Apparently, that donation included the agreement that Southern Baptist pastors would not have to pay for medical services in that hospital.

Decades after that transaction, I had a baby in that hospital. The cost for that baby was something like fifteen thousand dollars. For my husband and I at that time, it might as well have been fifteen million dollars. We couldn't pay it. I don't remember the exact amount, and the reason I don't remember is because one of the pastors my husband worked with told us, "Call the Baptist hospital, ask for the billing office, tell them that you're a Southern Baptist pastor, and they will wipe away your debt."

We couldn't believe it, but we called them, told them we owed thousands of dollars, that Brandon was a Southern Baptist pastor, and we asked them to forgive our debt. It took about thirty seconds, and they said "Okay, your account is at zero."

If we have accepted the work of Jesus in our place, that is what happens with the debt of our sin and shame. We just ask for our account to be cleared. "God, I heard that Jesus already took the punishment for my sin and that He's already canceled my shame; will You forgive it?" And the answer is always yes because the work is already done.

We were overwhelmed by that phone call and still talk about it today because we understood the magnitude of the bill. And we can't understand all the benefits we have from God if we don't understand our guilt and if we don't know how to release it in Him.

READ ROMANS 8:1-4. If you're new to Christianity, it's a lot of big words and potentially confusing language, I know. I don't want that to trip you up.

Read the first four verses slowly in whatever Bible you're using, and then write down anything that stands out to you below.

Here is that same passage in a translation that might be easier to understand.

> ***The Solution Is Life on God's Terms***
>
> *With the arrival of Jesus, the Messiah, that fateful dilemma is resolved. Those who enter into Christ's being-here-for-us no longer have to live under a continuous, low-lying black cloud. A new power is in operation. The Spirit of life in Christ, like a strong wind, has magnificently cleared the air, freeing you from a fated lifetime of brutal tyranny at the hands of sin and death.*
>
> *God went for the jugular when he sent his own Son. He didn't deal with the problem as something remote and unimportant. In his Son, Jesus, he personally took on the human condition, entered the disordered mess of struggling humanity in order to set it right once and for all. The law code, weakened as it always was by fractured human nature, could never have done that.*
>
> *The law always ended up being used as a Band-Aid on sin instead of a deep healing of it. And now what the law code asked for but we couldn't deliver is accomplished as we, instead of redoubling our own efforts, simply embrace what the Spirit is doing in us.*
>
> ROMANS 8:1-4, THE MESSAGE

I don't know Greek or Hebrew (don't worry, the editors of this study do), so I love looking at the same passage in multiple translations. (You can do this free online at biblegateway.com, blueletterbible.org, and biblehub.com.)

Seeing the same thing said in a new way often helps it click for me. The law was a Band-Aid®, but Jesus Christ heals us deeply. "Redoubling our efforts" is not going to take away from how badly we've messed everything up. Embracing the Spirit is what will make us new. How beautiful.

The law in this case was referring to the law God gave Moses in the Old Testament. The Jewish people were still looking to the law for salvation and instructions for right living. Jesus came to fulfill the law for us (Matt. 5:17). Today we don't often think of the law of Moses, but we do often try to live by our own set of rules, whether that means the law of the government, what we consider to be the rules of being a good Christian, or a set of demands we've created in our own minds to live right.

What has it looked like in your own life when you tried to live by the law?

When did you realize you couldn't do it?

READ ROMANS 8:5-11. **What is the mindset of the Spirit?**

What hope! We are no longer in the flesh if we have made the decision to follow Christ. We have life and peace. While our bodies will still experience death here on earth, we have a future resurrection to look forward to and a present life in abundance (John 10:10) to live in now.

What are the most meaningful ways you have embraced the Spirit who makes you new?

Today, pray that God will help you embrace and enjoy life in His Spirit. Ask Him to help you turn from striving and trying to be good on your own. Ask Him to forgive your mistakes and make you into a more joyful, more peaceful worshiper of Him.

DAY FOUR

REASSURANCE FOR US LITTLE CHILDREN

1 John 2:28–29; 3:1–24

Becoming a mom has changed how I think about the second coming. Here's what I mean. Today, as I'm finishing up the draft of this study, my youngest daughter has been learning to knit a scarf. It's not a perfect scarf, but she did improbably great on her first try. Seeing her wear it is too adorable. And this afternoon, all I wanted in the world was for her to succeed at her first attempt at knitting. Because her sadness is my sadness. Her frustrations are mine. Her pain gives me pain. I would never watch my baby knit and hope for the worst. I only hope for the best. I want to see her thrive. I want to see her joyful. I want to see her knit with the power of a thousand grannies. So, I would never, ever wish for her to fail. I don't watch her try things hoping for a chance to call her out. I love her. She's mine. And I'm an imperfect mom. I'm a flawed knitter nurturer.

But our God is a PERFECT Father. So, please let this into your heart: God is not waiting for you to mess up. He's not hoping to see you sin right before He comes again. When He comes in the clouds, it won't be a cosmic-level "gotcha" for all His followers who failed most recently. He's not hanging out in heaven waiting for you to botch your scarf before He blows the trumpet and returns to shame you. Your sadness is His sadness. Your pain does not go unnoticed. God cares for the brokenhearted (Ps. 34:18).

He loves us. We're His. So I love how John addresses his readers as "little children" in his letter. Yes, God has the right to judge all the evil and all the failure in the world, and He will. But the judge is our Dad. We are His little daughters. He wants to see us thrive forever. Amazing.

READ 1 JOHN 2:28-29. **According to these verses, what are we supposed to do so that we are not "ashamed" when Christ returns?**

READ 1 JOHN 3:1-3. **What does verse 1 show us is the great love of God?**

What do we know about everyone who has this hope in God, based on verse 3?

We who are children of God are pure. We're pure! No matter how dirty your life has been, no matter how dark, no matter how far you've walked from God. No matter what you can remember from your past. If you are His child, He purifies you like He is pure.

READ 1 JOHN 3:4-10. **Do these verses feel confusing or contradictory in light of what you read just a few verses ago? Explain.**

These verses can be confusing if you're a former or current striver, like me. I remember being baffled and anxious when Jesus or His disciples wrote about how we are to live as children of God. I'm going to mess that up! I've already messed that up!

But you have to remember the overarching message of the gospel, which is that we cannot and did not earn our purity. It was a free gift, and because we have been so loved, so forgiven, and so blessed, the Spirit of God changes us and makes us holier.

My husband has often preached, "If you read God's Word and don't feel hopeful, keep reading."

So, let's keep reading. *READ 1 JOHN 3:11-24.* What is John urging us "little children" to do in verse 18?

Our good works are a sign of our salvation, not a means to it. John is urging believers to live out our position in Jesus, not like the Jewish religious leaders of the day who knew the law and could speak the law but didn't live the law. No. Real believers will love "in action and in truth." It is a result of our conversion. It's a result of God's love for us. Let's keep reading.

***COPY DOWN 1 JOHN 3:19-20* in big bold letters in the space below. Underline what will happen to our hearts.**

I'm going to type it out and underline it here, too.

> *This is how we will know that we belong to the truth and will reassure our hearts before him whenever our hearts condemn us; for God is greater than our hearts, and he knows all things.*

I don't know about you, but when I battle shame, what I long for most is reassurance. I want to know that I'm okay. I want to know that the shame I'm wrestling with today doesn't condemn me.

So, how can we be reassured? It's right there in your handwriting above. GOD IS GREATER THAN OUR HEARTS. When your heart condemns you, God says, "There is now no condemnation for those in Christ Jesus" (Rom. 8:1).

Who is greater? No brainer. God is greater than your heart. He's greater than your memories, your shame, your internal condemnation. He wants to interrupt your shame reel with a commercial of Jesus saying, "It is finished" (John 19:30). God is always greater than your heart. And the more you reflect on that, the more your life will reflect Jesus's life, and as it does, you will see and know and be reassured that you are a child of God.

Consider writing out those verses on an index card or sticky note and placing it wherever your shame reel starts playing in your head—your mirror, your car dashboard, above your kitchen sink—as a reminder that God is greater.

READ 1 JOHN 3:21-24. **What are we commanded to do?**

Close out this day reflecting on what it might look like for you to obey God today. Walking in a relationship with Jesus leads to obedience. Obedience leads to joy and reassurance. There's no more room for shame when you're full of joy.

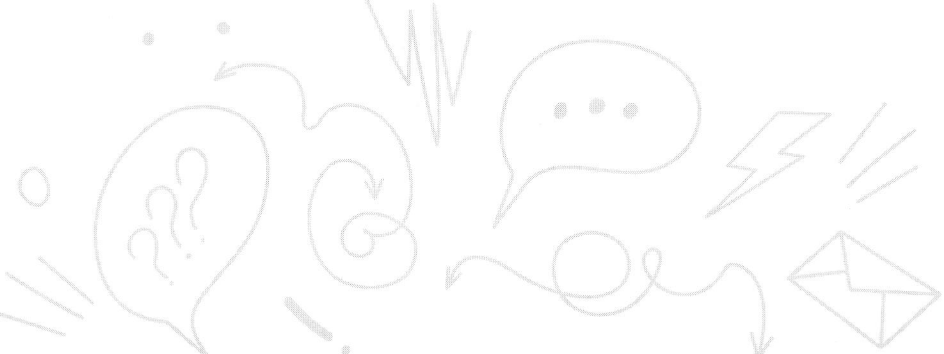

DAY FIVE

IN A CLOUD OF RIGHTEOUS COMPANY

Hebrews 11:32–12:3

READ HEBREWS 11:32-40. **Do you recognize any of those Bible names from the Old Testament? What do you remember about them besides what was listed in these verses?**

What does verse 39 say they were approved "through"?

I heard Bible stories growing up and viewed all the people as heroes. But if you actually read their stories, they had big-time failures too. Plenty to be ashamed of. First on that list is Gideon. We usually stop talking about him after God uses him to defeat the Midianites. But do you know how his story ends? Check out Judges 8:27:

> *Gideon made an ephod from all this and put it in Ophrah, his hometown. Then all Israel prostituted themselves by worshiping it there, and it became a snare to Gideon and his household.*

Gideon got to rescue God's people, then his life ended shamefully and "the Israelites did not remember the LORD their God who had rescued them from the hand of the enemies around them" (v. 34). That's not just the end of Gideon's shame reel, that's the end of his life reel.

David, number five on the list, was an adulterer who had someone murdered. But, of course, he also defeated a giant through God's power and won victories for God's people.

The "Hall of Faith" is filled with failure-heroes. This is such a relief, isn't it? We can be used big time for God even though we fail. Shameful moments don't disqualify us. Jesus's perfection qualifies us.

And that is the incredible reality we have in Jesus. Because of Jesus, we can have a powerful impact in this world. But because of Jesus, we don't actually have to save the day. Jesus has already saved the day. Jesus is mighty enough to lead us to incredible impact, and Jesus is mighty enough to cover incredible failures. Our approval then is based on the Object of our faith, not our perfect track record.

LOOK AT HEBREWS 12:1-3. **The writer of Hebrews urges us to do a few things in light of this great "cloud of witnesses" he just wrote about in chapter 11. What does he say to do? Finish these sentences.**

We are to lay aside ______________________________

We are to run with ______________________________

We are to keep our eyes on ______________________________

Now, personalize it. What could it practically look like to do those three things in your own life?

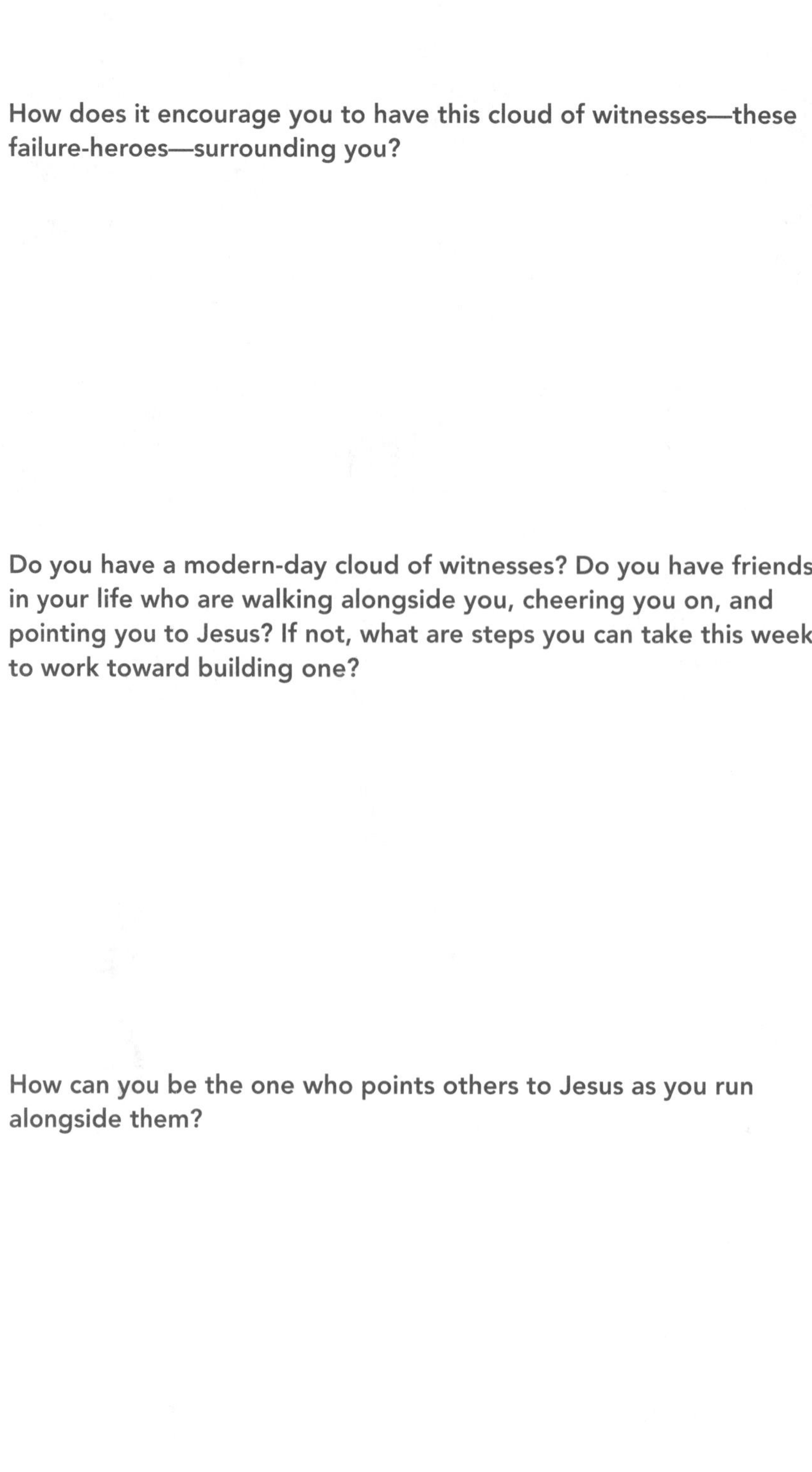

How does it encourage you to have this cloud of witnesses—these failure-heroes—surrounding you?

Do you have a modern-day cloud of witnesses? Do you have friends in your life who are walking alongside you, cheering you on, and pointing you to Jesus? If not, what are steps you can take this week to work toward building one?

How can you be the one who points others to Jesus as you run alongside them?

Jesus is the pioneer and perfecter of our faith. He wore your shame and suffered your punishment and conquered it. He is at God's right hand right now (Rom. 8:34), preparing a place for you (John 14:2).

> *Your shame was crucified when Jesus was. It's finished. Our hope was established when He rose from the dead. Hallelujah! We don't have to live with shame. We are forgiven.*

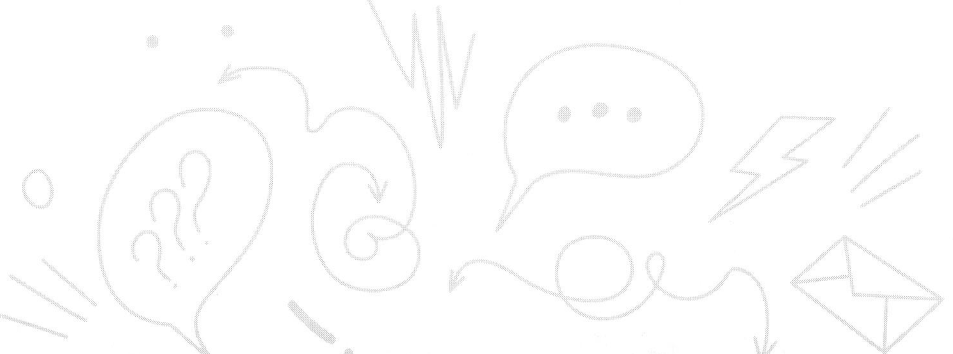

WATCH

Write down any thoughts, verses, or things you want to remember as you watch the video for Session Six.

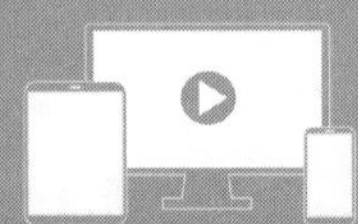

To access the video teaching sessions, use the instructions in the back of your Bible study book.

WATCH

Write down any thoughts, verses, or things you want to remember as you watch the video for Session Six.

DISCUSS

This week, we looked at shame and why we don't have to live enslaved to it. We were reminded through New Testament writers, inspired by the Holy Spirit, that we are justified and pure and righteous because of our faith in Jesus. Is this concept difficult for you to grasp or remember? Why or why not?

This session's main idea is "Jesus experienced our shame so we don't have to." Take a few minutes to talk about what that means and why it matters for us today.

On Day Five, you personalized Hebrews 12:1-3. What can living out those verses look like for you and what might it look like for the group?

What is the number one thing you have taken away from this study over the past six weeks?

PRAY

Thank God for His Word and its shame-fighting power. Ask that He'd continue the good work He's done in you and your group as you continue to walk with Him.

FROM THIS WEEK'S STUDY

Review this week's memory verse.

Therefore, since we also have such a large cloud of witnesses surrounding us, let us lay aside every hindrance and the sin that so easily ensnares us. Let us run with endurance the race that lies before us, keeping our eyes on Jesus, the pioneer and perfecter of our faith. For the joy that lay before him, he endured the cross, despising the shame, and sat down at the right hand of the throne of God.

HEBREWS 12:1-2

LEADING A GROUP?

A free leader guide PDF is available for download at **lifeway.com/ashamed**

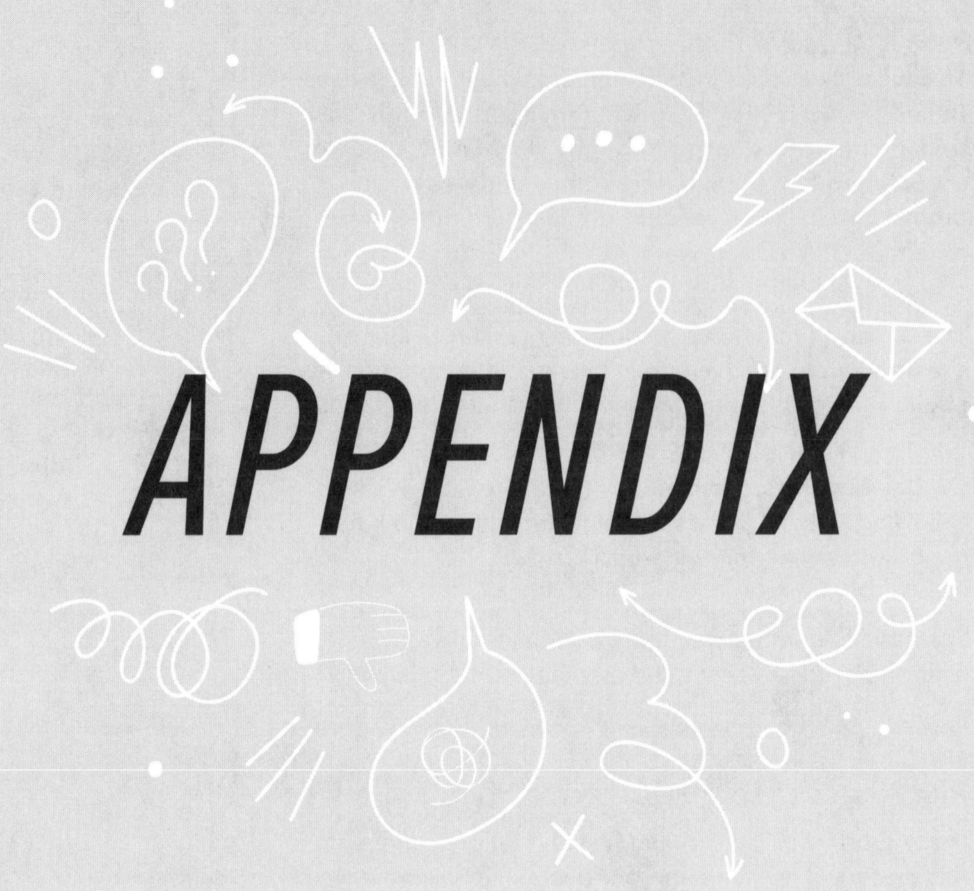

APPENDIX

BECOMING A CHRISTIAN

Romans 10:17 says, "So faith comes from what is heard, and what is heard comes through the message about Christ."

Maybe you've stumbled across new information in this study. Maybe you've attended church all your life, but something you read here struck you differently than it ever has before. Or maybe you are exhausted from wrestling with shame, and you are looking for the rest and peace that can only come from casting your cares on Jesus, who cares for you. If you have never accepted Christ but would like to, read on to discover how you can become a Christian.

Your heart tends to run from God and rebel against Him. The Bible calls this sin. Romans 3:23 says, "For all have sinned and fall short of the glory of God."

Yet God loves you and wants to save you from sin, to offer you a new life of hope. John 10:10b says, "I have come so that they may have life and have it in abundance."

To give you this gift of salvation, God made a way through His Son, Jesus Christ. Romans 5:8 says, "But God proves his own love for us in that while we were still sinners, Christ died for us."

You receive this gift by faith alone. Ephesians 2:8-9 says, "For you are saved by grace through faith, and this is not from yourselves; it is God's gift—not from works, so that no one can boast."

Faith is a decision of your heart demonstrated by the actions of your life. Romans 10:9 says, "If you confess with your mouth, 'Jesus is Lord,' and believe in your heart that God raised him from the dead, you will be saved."

If you trust that Jesus died for your sins and want to receive new life through Him, pray a prayer similar to the following one to express your repentance and faith in Him.

Dear God, I know I am a sinner. I believe Jesus died to forgive me of my sins. I accept Your offer of eternal life. Thank You for forgiving me of all my sins. Thank You for my new life. From this day forward, I will choose to follow You.

If you have trusted Jesus for salvation, please share your decision with your group leader or another Christian friend. If you are not already attending church, find one in which you can worship and grow in your faith. Following Christ's example, ask to be baptized as a public expression of your faith.

SCARLET'S FAVORITE SHAME-FIGHTING VERSES

A lot of these verses have been pulled from what we've studied the last few weeks, so you know some of the context. If a verse is new to you (or even if you have heard it before), I would encourage you to read the context around the verse. That way, you can more fully understand what it is about. This is the Word of God! Put these in your pocket. Tape them to your mirrors. Write them on your children's faces! This is truth. These words have power. This is how we fight.

But you, LORD, are a shield around me,
my glory, and the one who lifts up my head.

PSALM 3:3

4 I sought the LORD, and he answered me
and rescued me from all my fears.
5 Those who look to him are radiant with joy;
their faces will never be ashamed.

PSALM 34:4-5

As far as the east is from the west,
so far has he removed
our transgressions from us.

PSALM 103:12

The Lord GOD will help me;
therefore I have not been humiliated;
therefore I have set my face like flint,
and I know I will not be put to shame.

ISAIAH 50:7

4 "Do not be afraid, for you will not be put to shame;
don't be humiliated, for you will not be disgraced.
For you will forget the shame of your youth,
and you will no longer remember
the disgrace of your widowhood.
5 Indeed, your husband is your Maker —
his name is the LORD of Armies —
and the Holy One of Israel is your Redeemer;
he is called the God of the whole earth.
6 For the LORD has called you,
like a wife deserted and wounded in spirit,
a wife of one's youth when she is rejected,"
says your God.
7 "I deserted you for a brief moment,
but I will take you back with abundant compassion.
8 In a surge of anger
I hid my face from you for a moment,
but I will have compassion on you
with everlasting love,"
says the LORD your Redeemer.

ISAIAH 54:4-8

In place of your shame, you will have a double portion;
in place of disgrace, they will rejoice over their share.
So they will possess double in their land,
and eternal joy will be theirs.

ISAIAH 61:7

He will again have compassion on us; he will vanquish our iniquities.
You will cast all our sins into the depths of the sea.

MICAH 7:19

Therefore, there is now no condemnation for those in Christ Jesus.

ROMANS 8:1

For the Scripture says, Everyone who believes on him will not be put to shame.

ROMANS 10:11

For godly grief produces a repentance that leads to salvation without regret, but worldly grief produces death.

2 CORINTHIANS 7:10

How much more will the blood of Christ, who through the eternal Spirit offered himself without blemish to God, cleanse our consciences from dead works so that we can serve the living God?

HEBREWS 9:14

Let us draw near with a true heart in full assurance of faith, with our hearts sprinkled clean from an evil conscience and our bodies washed in pure water.

HEBREWS 10:22

. . . keeping our eyes on Jesus, the pioneer and perfecter of our faith. For the joy that lay before him, he endured the cross, despising the shame, and sat down at the right hand of the throne of God.

HEBREWS 12:2

But if anyone suffers as a Christian, let him not be ashamed but let him glorify God in having that name.

1 PETER 4:16

NOTES

NOTES

NOTES

ENDNOTES

SESSION TWO

1. Strong's H5771: aôn, Blue Letter Bible, accessed May 22, 2023, https://www.blueletterbible.org/lexicon/h5771/csb/wlc/0-1/.

2. Andrew M. Davis, *Exalting Jesus in Isaiah* (Nashville, TN: Holman Reference, 2017), 41.

3. J. R. R. Tolkien, *The Return of the King* (New York: Harper Collins, 1967), 283.

4. A. W. Tozer, *The Knowledge of the Holy* (New York: HarperOne, 1961), 70.

SESSION THREE

1. D. A. Carson, *The Gospel According to John, The Pillar New Testament Commentary* (Leicester, England; Grand Rapids, MI: Inter-Varsity Press; W.B. Eerdmans, 1991), 216.

SESSION FOUR

1. Thabiti Anyabwile, *Christ-Centered Exposition Commentary: Exalting Jesus in Luke* (Nashville: B&H Publishing Group, 2018).

2. A. Boyd Luter, "Galatians," in *CSB Study Bible: Notes*, ed. Edwin A. Blum and Trevin Wax (Nashville, TN: Holman Bible Publishers, 2017), 1860.

3. Edward T. Welch, *When People are Big and God is Small* (Phillipsburg, New Jersey: P & R Publishing, 2023), ch. 1.

4. Ashley Hamer, "Here's Why Smells Trigger Such Vivid Memories," *Discovery*, August 1, 2019, https://www.discovery.com/science/Why-Smells-Trigger-Such-Vivid-Memories.

5. Timothy Keller, *The Reason for God* (New York: Penguin Books, 2008), ch. 11.

ALSO AVAILABLE FROM

SCARLET HILTIBIDAL

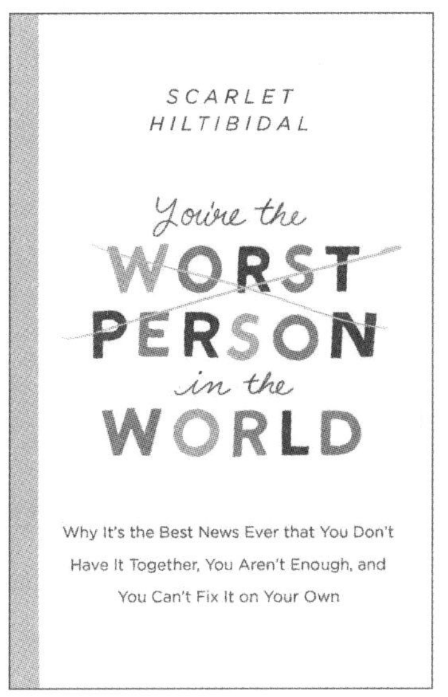

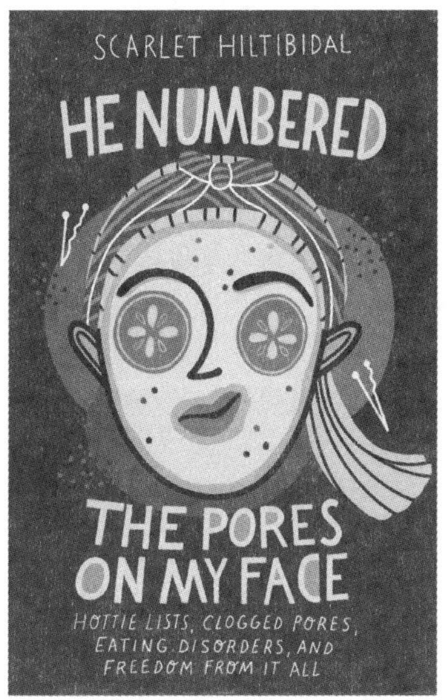

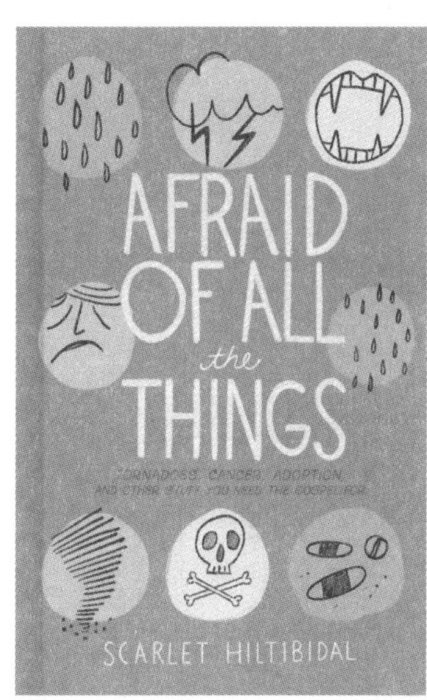

FOR TEENS

Available wherever books are sold

Get the most from your study.

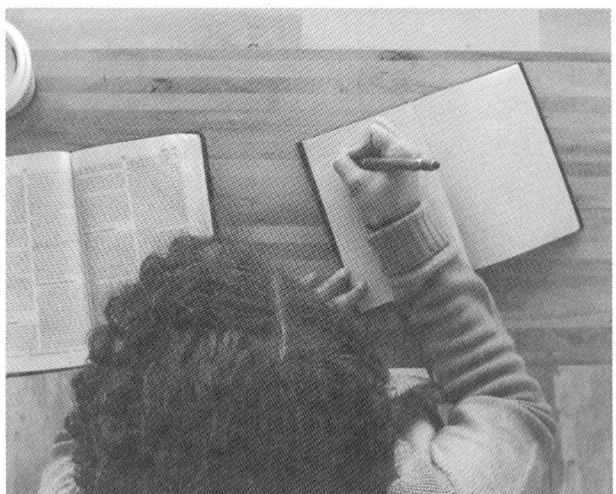

IN THIS STUDY, YOU'LL:

- Gain perspective on sources of shame and grasp a vision for how to find freedom through God's Word.
- Experience the miraculous shift of living in light of the gospel today rather than hoping for a happy someday.
- Learn from the stories of women and men in the Bible who overcame their shame to walk in the freedom of God.

To enrich your study experience, consider the accompanying video teaching sessions from Scarlet Hiltibidal, approximately 7 minutes each.

STUDYING ON YOUR OWN?

Watch Scarlet Hiltibidal's teaching sessions, available via redemption code for individual video-streaming access, printed in this Bible study book.

LEADING A GROUP?

Each group member will need an *Ashamed* study book, which includes video access. Because all participants will have access to the video content, you can choose to watch the videos outside of your group meeting if desired. Or, if you're watching together and someone misses a group meeting, they'll have the flexibility to catch up! A DVD set is also available to purchase separately if desired.

Plus, visit lifeway.com/ashamed to download a free leader guide that includes leader tips, a suggested schedule, and discussion questions to accompany each session of the study.

ADDITIONAL RESOURCES

DVD Set, includes 6 video teaching sessions from Scarlet Hiltibidal, each approximately 7 minutes

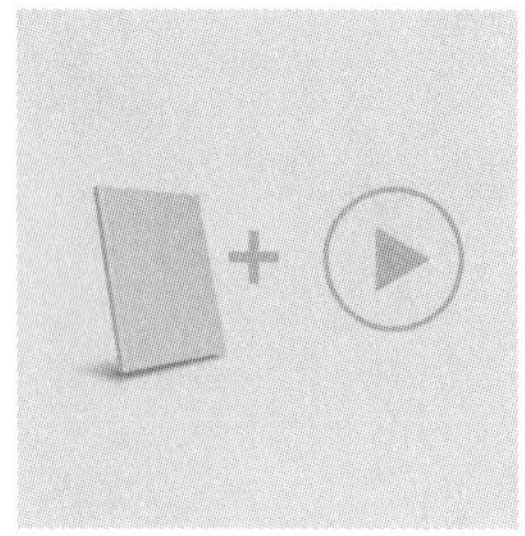

eBook with video access, includes 6 video teaching sessions from Scarlet Hiltibidal, each approximately 7 minutes

Browse study formats, a free session sample, a free leader guide, video clips, church promotional materials, and more at

lifeway.com/ashamed